EXCLUSIONARY INJUSTICE

POLITICAL SCIENCE AND PUBLIC ADMINISTRATION
A Program of Textbooks and Monographs

Executive Editors

KENNETH FRIEDMAN
Department of Political Science
Purdue University
West Lafayette, Indiana

NICHOLAS L. HENRY
Center for Public Affairs
Arizona State University
Tempe, Arizona

Further volumes in preparation

EXCLUSIONARY INJUSTICE

THE PROBLEM OF ILLEGALLY OBTAINED EVIDENCE

Steven R. Schlesinger

Department of Political Science
Rutgers University
Camden College of Arts and Sciences
Camden, New Jersey

MARCEL DEKKER, INC.   New York and Basel

Library of Congress Cataloging in Publication Data

Schlesinger, Steven R
    Exclusionary injustice.

    (Political science and public administration ; 3)
    Bibliography: p.
    Includes indexes.
    1. Admissions (Law)--United States. 2. Evidence,
Criminal--United States. 3. Searches and seizures--
United States. I. Title. II. Series.
KF9662.S34   345'.73'062   77-8287
ISBN 0-8247-6564-8

The author wishes to thank The Heritage Foundation, Inc.,
513 C Street, N.E., Washington, D.C. 20002 for use of
material from its publication.

MARCEL DEKKER, INC.
270 Madison Avenue, New York, New York 10016

Current printing (last digit):
10 9 8 7 6 5 4 3 2 1

PRINTED IN THE UNITED STATES OF AMERICA

To my Father and Mother

and

To my Wife

Contents

Acknowledgments

This book would not have been possible without the support and advice of my generous family, friends, and associates. Howard Rotblat, a law student at Rutgers University, Camden and my research assistant, did a great deal of library digging and was an excellent devil's advocate as I was formulating and refining the ideas in the book. My colleague, Jay Sigler, was a constant source of encouragement and helpful advice, and my department chairman, Harry Shapiro, gave me both the moral support and the freedom necessary to bring this project to completion.

My mother gave me large doses of maternal concern and encouragement at all times, but especially when my mood was foulest; my father, Rudolf B. Schlesinger, Professor at Hastings College of the Law, gave me the benefit of his vast erudition and superb insights in the countless hours of conversation we had about this book. My wife Madeline has advised me on every aspect of this project; she knows how greatly I value her contribution.

I wish to thank The Heritage Foundation, Inc. for permission to reprint or paraphrase large portions of my monograph, *Federalism and Criminal Justice: The Case of the Exclusionary Rule.* Also, I thank the *Journal of Legal Studies* and the *University of Chicago Law Review* for permission to reproduce tables and figures which originally appeared in these publications.

Kenneth Friedman, Purdue University, and Michael J. Malbin, *National Journal Reports,* made many helpful suggestions and criticisms.

I am grateful to Rutgers University for providing a Research Council summer grant in 1974 and a sabbatical leave in 1976; these gave me uninterrupted periods for research, reflection, and writing.

The author assumes sole responsibility for the shortcomings of this book.

Steven R. Schlesinger

EXCLUSIONARY
INJUSTICE

—————————CHAPTER 1—————————

The Exclusionary Rule—A Problematic
Response to Illegal Search and Seizure

The Fourth Amendment to the Constitution of the United States provides a "right of the people to be secure . . . against unreasonable searches and seizures . . . ." In an effort to apply and enforce that right, the Supreme Court of the United States has imposed the exclusionary rule upon federal courts since 1886 and upon state courts since 1961. The exclusionary rule is a rule of evidence which excludes, or renders inadmissable in a criminal proceeding, evidence that is illegally obtained by law enforcement officials. Thus, evidence obtained by an illegal search and seizure could not, under present Supreme Court holdings, be considered admissible in any criminal prosecution in the land. It makes no difference whether the evidence was secured in a legally debatable search—one which produces close and split opinions in appellate courts—or in a blatant and willful violation of the law by the police. The fruits of all police procedures judged to be illegal by the courts or legislatures must be excluded.[1]

The exclusionary rule affects four types of illegal activities undertaken by law enforcement officials[2]:

1. Illegal search and seizure. The search of a residence without a warrant, such as that documented in *Mapp v. Ohio*,[3] is an example of such illegal activity.

2. Confession secured by means contrary to the Fifth or Sixth Amendments. A confession secured in a police stationhouse without having fully apprised the suspect of his rights to remain silent and to be represented by counsel, would be an instance of illegally-obtained confession. *Miranda v. Arizona*[4] would be a case in point.

1

3. Securing of identification testimony in violation of the Fifth or Sixth Amendments. An improperly conducted police lineup, such as that revealed in *Gilbert v. California*,[5] would be an example of this.

4. Police methods that "shock the conscience," such as the involuntary stomach pumping associated with *Rochin v. California*.[6]

We will deal with the exclusionary rule primarily as it pertains to the first category, search and seizure. There are at least three reasons for this: The rule is most frequently invoked in search and seizure cases, through motions by defense counsel to suppress evidence.[7] Also, in order to support the arguments put forward in this essay, it is not necessary to refer to other areas in which the exclusionary rule is applied, such as confessions or identifications, which would require considerable additional legal background for the reader. In addition, the exclusion of illegally obtained confessions involves the consideration of the reliability of such confessions, which is irrelevant to the purpose of the rule as it pertains to search and seizure cases.

The Rule in Practice

In order to clarify the practical operation of the rule, let us suppose that a number of people have been brutally murdered; a police officer finds some physical evidence strongly indicating the guilt of a certain person, but the officer's search warrant is in some way deficient. The evidence is available to the court, but the court must refuse to consider it, and, if other evidence is insufficient for a conviction, the suspect is released.

> There are literally hundreds of persons guilty of narcotics and gun offenses who walk the streets, despite their obvious guilt, because the evidence essential to their conviction has been suppressed, and it's not limited to narcotics and gun cases. In one recent instance in my experience a person murdered a young teenage girl and hid her body in a rural farm area. The police got a warrant signed by a judge which gave them the right to search, but there was a technical deficiency in the warrant, and the Court held that the very body itself, the nature of the crime itself, had to be suppressed. It was a magical disappearing act. It was as if this young girl had never walked the earth.[8]

The case described above is not atypical. Oaks, in his important article "Studying the Exclusionary Rule in Search and Seizure" points out:

> ... evidence obtained by a search is likely to be vital to conviction in most types of crimes where searches are commonly involved (notably gambling, narcotics and weapons). Confessions are generally less vital. Thus the application of the exclusionary rule to evidence obtained by improper search and seizure is specially vulnerable to the criticism of freeing the guilty because it often excludes reliable (and often practically conclusive) evidence of guilt, and it frequently results in immediate termination of the prosecution.[9]

A case illustrating the dangerous results of the rule is the 1971 decision of the United States Supreme Court reversing a murder conviction where part of the evidence consisted of automobile vacuum sweepings seized without a warrant.[10] Thus, the exclusionary rule results in the freeing of many suspects whose cases contain probative evidence clearly pointing to guilt, or results in a new trial of these suspects in which significant, if not crucial, evidence may not be admitted.

A great deal of otherwise reliable evidence is not used in criminal prosecutions because of the operation of the rule. For example, a 1969 study of two Chicago circuit courts showed that during 12 sample days, 457 defendants were prosecuted for narcotics violations and 188 for carrying concealed weapons. Thirty-four percent of the narcotics prosecutions and 36% of the weapons prosecutions were met with motions to suppress (i.e., motions to exclude evidence). Of these, 97% of the narcotics motions and 68% of the weapons motions were granted.[11] In 1971, in three branches of Chicago circuit court, 2,060 defendants were prosecuted for narcotics violations and 929 for carrying concealed weapons. Forty-three percent of the narcotics prosecutions and 36% of the weapons prosecutions were met with motions to suppress evidence; 84% of the narcotics motions and 62% of the weapons motions were granted.[12]

These statistics suggest that a substantial number of otherwise guilty criminals escape likely conviction because of the application of the exclusionary rule and that police misconduct is the reason for such frequent application. Since the deterrence of police misbehavior is a major justification offered for the rule, these statistics cast doubt on the success of the rule as a deterrent. If the rule has not been a successful deterrent, then it is time to consider effective alternatives.

A Problem Whose Time Has Come

There are a number of reasons for studying the exclusionary rule at this time and for questioning whether it constitutes good public policy with respect to criminal justice. The operation of the rule in the United States is more extensive, by any standard (e.g., the amount of evidence excluded or the number of otherwise convictable suspects released) than it is in any other country in the world[13] (see Appendix II). We have, perhaps, gone too far with the use of the rule, particularly considering the substantial liabilities of extensive exclusion which are discussed in this and subsequent chapters.

At the present time, when this country is experiencing a dramatic increase in the crime rate, it is especially appropriate to ask whether extensive exclusion of evidence and a consequent loss of convictions is justifiable. In the 1960s, serious crimes committed in the United States increased 196.9% and the rate of offenses per 100,000 inhabitants increased 158.1%.[14] In 1970, there were 74,000 robberies reported in New York City alone.[15] In light of this information, it is doubtful whether a substantial limitation on law enforcement and prosecution such as the exclusionary rule can be justified.

Sharp and fundamental disagreement continues to exist within the Supreme Court concerning both the constitutional necessity for the rule and its wisdom from the point of view of public policy. The crucial *Mapp*[16] decision applying the rule to the states, the important decision in *Calandra*[17] limiting the scope of the rule at the grand jury level, and the recent decisions limiting the relief available in federal courts to state prisoners who claim search and seizure violations in their state trials,[18] produced sharp dissents from three or four justices. Basic disagreement within our highest judicial body concerning important matters of public policy should encourage thorough examination of the issues under scrutiny.

Another reason for reconsidering the rule now is that it is subject to review and modification by the Supreme Court; indeed, there are signs that the Court might soon consider modifying the rule. Recently, it held that improperly obtained confessions may be used under certain circumstances. In *Harris v. New York,* a six-member majority held that while statements made to police by a suspect who has not been advised of his rights cannot be introduced in a trial court for the prosecution's case in chief, they can be employed to impeach the credibility of the defendant should he testify on his own behalf.[19] Other recent cases carve out other circumstances in which improperly obtained confessions need not be excluded.[20] If the Court is willing to admit such unlawfully obtained evidence, what other types of illegally obtained evidence could be admitted? Principles developed in the confessions area may carry over to search and seizure. If the cases discussed above are a reliable guide, it is quite possible that the Supreme Court will continue to limit the scope of the rule when applying it to search and seizure, as it began to do in *Calandra.*[21]

In its 1975-76 term, the Supreme Court considered a case which raised the important question of whether the exclusionary rule should be applied in cases involving magisterial error in the issuing of a search warrant and, more generally, whether it should be applied in cases where police officers, acting in good faith, technically violated the Fourth Amendment.[22] The Court, however, decided this case on the basis of issues not related to magisterial error or police actions in good faith. Nonetheless, given the developments described in the previous paragraph, Chief Justice Burger's antipathy toward the rule expressed in his *Bivens* dissent[23] (see Appendix I) and the reservations expressed by a majority of the current Supreme Court in cases concerning grand juries and state prisoners seeking federal court relief,[24] it seems reasonable to expect, in future cases, the modification of earlier decisions, moving toward a further narrowing of the scope of the rule, or even its abolition. These developments argue that study of the rule is most timely.

Finally, there is much legal literature which seriously questions the value of the rule.[25] It raises fundamental questions about the deterrent effectiveness of the rule as to police misbehavior and argues that the rule actually encourages certain forms of police misbehavior such as perjury on the witness stand and corruption in the form of protecting certain suspects from conviction. It discusses the numerous liabilities not related to deterrence attached to the operation of the rule. These include: the release of many persons who would be convictable in the absence of the rule, the rule's lack of aid or compensation to innocent victims of illegal search and seizure, the tendency of the rule to decrease public respect for the legal and judicial system, the failure of the rule to distinguish between petty offenses and grave crimes or between willful, flagrant violations by police officers and those violations which are unintentional. The rule excludes the most credible kinds of evidence, it tends to intensify plea bargaining, and it contributes to dangerously enlarged notions of what constitutes proper searches and seizures. However, the rule does have defenders; both cases and law review literature abound with defenses of the rule.[26] This literature argues that the rule has achieved substantial success as a deterrent against illegal police behavior and that it protects privacy and the due process guarantees of the Fifth and Fourteenth Amendments.

The Argument and Proposed Remedy

The argument made in this book is that we must recognize the liabilities of the exclusionary rule and be prepared, after examination, to reevaluate present policy. More than a decade of experience has shown that the rule does little to deter official misconduct. Certainly, it does not offer aid, compensation, or any meaningful remedy to the innocent victims of official misconduct. To put the matter in clearest form, present policy determines that in any case where a criminal court must deal with a possibility guilty criminal and the clearly errant officer who apprehended him, it should acquit its responsibility by punishing or disciplining neither. A rule so contrary to reason and sound public policy is an incongruity in the American legal system that warrants examination. We must be prepared to stop clinging to a seemingly unworkable and possibly irrational rule of law when there are alternatives which may succeed in deterring police misconduct at least as well as the rule, without many of its dangerous shortcomings and side effects. We will propose such an alternative which, it is argued, merits serious consideration.

We do not propose that the Court simply abandon the exclusionary rule with no substitute designed to deter official misconduct, for that would mean that a kind of open season had been declared on criminal suspects. Our federal system presents us with 50 states, some of which would surely be greatly encouraged to try different methods of deterring police misconduct if the Supreme Court gave state legislatures a choice between the rule and some other method of deterrence. Such diversity would give us needed information that would enable us to assess the exclusionary rule in competition with its alternatives. Indeed, such experiments may show that some other means are more attractive than either the rule or the proposals made here to substitute for it. However, at present we know very little about the effectiveness of alternatives to the rule. If we take advantage of the diversity of experience and information that would be created by allowing the primary units of our federal system, the states, to try other methods of deterring police misbehavior, our federal system can help us move away from the exclusionary rule in a reasonable fashion.

The book is organized in four chapters. This brief introduction is followed by a history of the development of the exclusionary rule in American Supreme Court jurisprudence. This history of the rule is discussed in the context of Supreme Court cases rather than the decisions of lower federal or state courts because the rationales and public policy considerations underlying the rule have been most fully and definitively explored in the High Court. Chapter 3 presents a series of arguments indicating that the two major public policy justifications advanced for the rule, protection of privacy and deterrence of illegal activity by law enforcement officials, cannot be sustained. An argument showing how the rule in fact encourages certain forms of police misbehavior noted earlier is included, followed by detailed discussion of the various other costs of the rule noted above. An examination of a proposed alternative to the rule which involves a combination of financial recovery for the innocent victim of illegal search and seizure and disciplinary action against the misbehaving officer(s) is given in Chapter 4. It is argued that this proposed alternative would constitute better public policy than the present rule.

Notes

1. The Supreme Court first imposed the rule on the federal courts in *Boyd v. United States,* 116 U.S. 616 (1886). Thereafter, the High Court had occasion to consider the rule or aspects of it in: *Weeks v. United States,* 232 U.S. 383 (1914); *Burdeau v. McDowell,* 256 U.S. 465 (1921); *Wolf v. Colorado,* 338 U.S. 25 (1949); *Rochin v. California,* 388 U.S. 263 (1957); *Mapp v. Ohio,* 367 U.S. 643 (1961); *Bivens v. Six Unknown Named Agents,* 403 U.S. 388 (1971); *United States v. Calandra,* 414 U.S. 338 (1974); and *Stone v. Powell,* 44 L.W. 5313 (1976). In the *Mapp* decision, the Court laid down the fundamental rule for the state courts: Any evidence obtained by search and seizure in violation of the Federal Constitution is inadmissable in a criminal trial in a state court. See Chapter 2 for a detailed history of the rule in the United States.

2. See Oaks, *Studying the Exclusionary Rule in Search and Seizure,* 37 U. Chi. L. Rev. 665, 665 (1970).

3. Footnote 1, *supra.*

4. 384 U.S. 436 (1966).

5. 388 U.S. 263 (1967).

6. Footnote 1, *supra.*

7. *Comment, Search and Seizure in Illinois: Enforcement of the Constitutional Right of Privacy,* 47 Nw. U. L. Rev. 493, 498 (1952).

8. Transcript of *"The Advocates,"* a Public Broadcasting Service (P.B.S.) program produced by WGBH—Boston, program taped March 4, 1974, 9-10, remarks of Mr. James Zagel, Director of the Criminal Justice Division of the Illinois Attorney General's Office.

9. Oaks, footnote 2, *supra,* 738. The empirical data supporting these conclusions is in Oaks, 681-689.

10. *Coolidge v. New Hampshire,* 403 U.S. 443 (1971).

11. Oaks, footnote 2, *supra,* 685.

12. Spiotto, *Search and Seizure: An Empirical Study of the Exclusionary Rule and Its Alternatives,* 2 J. Legal Studies 243, 247 (1973). The source of the data is Oaks, footnote 2, *supra,* 685.

13. *The Exclusionary Rule Regarding Illegally Seized Evidence: An International Symposium,* 52 J. Crim. L., C. and P.S. 245-292 (1961).
14. Hindelang, *et al., Sourcebook on Criminal Justice Statistics, 1973,* Law Enforcement Assistance Administration, U.S. Dept. of Justice, 198 (1973).
15. See Elliot, *Crime, Punishment and Professional Paradigms,* a paper delivered at the Annual Meeting of the American Political Science Association, Washington, D.C., 1972.
16. Footnote 1, *supra.*
17. *Ibid.* Most of the cases concerning the rule from 1960 to the present were decided by either one or two votes. These are discussed in Chapter 2.
18. *Wolff v. Rice,* 44 L.W. 5313 (1976) and *Stone v. Powell,* 44 L.W. 5313 (1976).
19. 401 U.S. 222 (1971).
20. See *Michigan v. Tucker,* 417 U.S. 433 (1974) and *Oregon v. Hass,* 420 U.S. 714 (1975).
21. Footnote 1, *supra.*
22. *Wolff v. Rice,* footnote 18, *supra.*
23. Footnote 1, *supra,* 411 (Burger, C. J., dissenting).
24. *Ibid.* See also *Wolff v. Rice* and *Stone v. Powell,* footnote 18, *supra.*
25. See, for example Barrett, *Exclusion of Evidence Obtained by Illegal Searches—A Comment on People v. Cahan,* 43 Calif. L. Rev. 565 (1965); Burns, *Mapp v. Ohio: An All-American Mistake,* 19 DePaul L. Rev. 80 (1961); Cox, *The Decline of the Exclusionary Rule: An Alternative to Injustice,* 4 Sw. U. L. Rev. 68 (1972); Friendly, *The Bill of Rights as a Code of Criminal Procedure,* 53 Calif. L. Rev. 929, 951-954 (1965); Satlin, *An Alternative to the Exclusionary Rule,* 26 JAG J. 255 (1972); Inbau, *Restrictions in the Law of Interrogations and Confessions,* 52 Nw. U. L. Rev. 77 (1958); Inbau, Thompson and Sowle, *Cases and Comments on Criminal Justice: Criminal Law Administration,* 1-84 (1968); Lafave, *Improving Police Performance Through the Exclusionary Rule (pts. 1 and 2),* 30 Mo. L. Rev. 391, 566 (1965); Lafave and Remington, *Controlling the Police: The Judge's Role in Making and Reviewing Law Enforcement Decisions,* 63 Mich. L. Rev. 987 (1965); Morris & Hawkins, *The Honest Politician's Guide to Crime Control,* 101 (1970); *Effect of Mapp v. Ohio on Police Search and Seizure Practice in Narcotics Cases,* 4 Colum. J. L. and Soc. Prob. 87 (1968); Oaks, *Studying the Exclusionary Rule in Search and Seizure,* footnote 2, *supra;* Plumb, *Illegal Enforcement of the Law,* 24 Cornell L. Q. 337 (1939); Schaefer, *The Fourteenth Amendment and the Sanctity of the Person,* 64 Nw. U. L. Rev. 1 (1969); *Student Comments: The Tort Alternative to the Exclusionary*

Rule in Search and Seizure, 63 J. Crim. L., C. and P.S. 256 (1972);
Waite, *Judges and the Crime Burden,* 54 Mich. L. Rev. 169 (1955);
Wigmore, *Using Evidence Obtained by Illegal Search and Seizure,* 8
ABA J. 479 (1922); 8 Wigmore, *Evidence,* section 2184a (McNaughton
rev., 1961); Wingo, *Growing Disillusionment with the Exclusionary
Rule,* 25 Sw. L. J. 573 (1971); *The Exclusionary Rule Regarding
Illegally Seized Evidence: An International Symposium,* footnote 13,
supra, 245-92. Each of the major criticisms of the rule contained in
the above literature are discussed and analyzed in this book. As each
criticism appears in the text we have provided numerous cross refer-
ences (in footnotes) to the literature cited above.

26. See especially, *Mapp v. Ohio,* footnote 1, *supra; Wolf v. Colorado,*
footnote 1, *supra,* 41 (Murphy and Rutledge, J. J., dissenting; Canon,
*Is the Exclusionary Rule In Failing Health? Some New Data and a
Plea Against A Precipitous Conclusion,* 62 Ky. L. J. 681 (1973-74);
*Critique, On the Limitations of Empirical Evaluations of the Exclu-
sionary Rule: A Critique of the Spiotto Research and United States
v. Calandra,* 69 Nw. U. L. Rev. 740 (1974).

CHAPTER 2

The Supreme Court As Chief Constable

The Supreme Court's leading decisions involving the exclusionary rule in search and seizure cases will be reviewed in this chapter. Such a review provides legal and informational background for the discussion of public policy in Chapters 3 and 4 and also helps to outline the dimensions of the problem of suppression of evidence in America. The cases discussed in this chapter are in chronological order, to give the reader a sense of the development of the suppression doctrine. The arguments of the justices concerning the appropriateness of suppression as a remedy for illegal official behavior are quoted extensively since they are germane to the public policy questions to be examined later. Table 1 presents the most important of the cases under consideration and the precedents established. Before beginning our discussion of the development of the American exclusionary rule in search and seizure cases, it is necessary briefly to sketch the state of American law on search and seizure.

The Rules Governing Proper Searches and Seizures

The Fourth Amendment to the Constitution provides that "The right of the people to be secure in their persons, houses, papers and effects, against unreasonable searches and seizures shall not be violated, and no Warrants shall issue, but upon probable cause, supported by Oath or affirmation, and particularly describing the place to be searched, and the persons or things to be seized." The terms of the Amendment clearly suggest that reasonable searches are permitted; only unreasonable ones are proscribed. Also, in general, searches should be conducted with a warrant.

 The Supreme Court has been obliged to deal with the problem of what

4th
Am

Table 1 Landmark Cases

Date	Case	Decision of the Supreme Court
1886	*Boyd v. United States*	First occasion on which Court ordered illegally seized evidence excluded
1914	*Weeks v. United States*	Reasserted the exclusionary rule for federal courts
1949	*Wolf v. Colorado*	Refused to impose the exclusionary rule on the states
1961	*Mapp v. Ohio*	Imposed the exclusionary rule on the states
1963	*Wong Sun v. United States*	Extended the exclusionary rule to include the "fruits" of an illegal search
1965	*Linkletter v. United States*	Refused to apply *Mapp* retroactively to cases decided before 1961
1974	*United States v. Calandra*	Refused to extend the exclusionary rule to grand jury questions based on illegally seized evidence
1976	*Wolff v. Rice* *Stone v. Powell*	Limited the relief available in federal courts for state prisoners who claim search and seizure violations in their state trials

constitutes a "reasonable" search and seizure and has held searches and seizures to be reasonable if (1) they are based upon a warrant issued by a magistrate; (2) the law enforcement officers demonstrate to that magistrate probable cause to believe that evidence of criminal activity will be brought to light by the requested search; (3) the request for a search warrant by the police to the magistrate includes some evidence other than the statements of the police that there is probable cause to believe that criminal activity will be uncovered; and (4) the warrant describes in sufficient detail the material to be searched for and seized.[1] The requirement of particularity came into American law partly as a reflection of the hatred for the "writs of assistance" under which British officers searched homes for contraband during the colonial period.

However, an officer does not need a warrant to search in situations where searches and seizures are incident to a lawful arrest. An officer may search (without a warrant) incident to a lawful arrest if he needs to search a suspect in order to remove dangerous weapons and thus protect his own safety, *or* if the officer needs to seize evidence which, if not seized, might be removed by the suspect. The relevant cases indicate that searches of a suspect's person are almost always justified if they are incident to a lawful arrest. In addition, searches of a suspect's person are justified, even though not incident to a lawful arrest, if the officer has probable cause to believe the suspect is armed. Searches of the location where the suspect is found must be limited to that area from which he might obtain a weapon or destroy evidence; officers may search only that area under the immediate control of the suspect, and may seize only that evidence which is in plain sight of the officer. Finally, the police need not obtain search warrants when the person whose home or possessions are to be searched has given consent. Such persons must, however, be warned that the fruits of the search may be used against them at trial.[2]

A police officer may employ "reasonable" force in carrying out a search; he may break down a door if he has been refused admission after giving clear notice of his authority and purpose.[3] Furthermore, police may enter a house in "hot pursuit" of a suspect without giving notice and search the house for the suspect, his weapons, and the fruits of the crime. Such hot pursuit may include chasing a suspect from a public place (his doorway), where the police initially see him, into a private place (his house).[4] The right to search an automobile on probable cause without a warrant has been recognized by the Court for over 50 years. Very recently, the Court held that officers may search the person of a driver incident to his arrest if his vehicle has been stopped for any lawful reason, and that a closed automobile glove compartment may be searched in the course of making an inventory of the objects in a car impounded for parking violations.[5] The Court has generally given police more leeway in searches of cars than of homes in consideration of the fact that a citizen does not traditionally feel entitled to the same degree of privacy while in his car that he would while in his own home.

When officers have a valid search warrant, they may seize any and all contraband in plain sight within the area designated by the warrant, regardless of whether the specific type of contraband is named in the warrant.[6]

Finally, police officers must not judge for themselves the necessity of a search when there is time to obtain a warrant from a magistrate, for the purpose of bringing a magistrate into the proceedings is to exert a detached and neutral influence. Specifically, an officer's belief that evidence exists to justify a search warrant does not justify him in executing a warrantless search.[7]

Items seized in improperly conducted searches may, under the exclusionary rule, be excluded at the defendant's trial on motion of defense counsel. It is to the development of the exclusionary rule by the Supreme Court that we now turn.

The Development of the Exclusionary Rule

The Early Federal Cases

Any chronological review of Supreme Court search and seizure cases involving invocation of the exclusionary rule must begin in 1886 with *Boyd v. United States.* [8] This was the first occasion on which the Court ordered the exclusion of evidence that the justices found to have been illegally obtained. The High Court overruled a trial court which had upheld a statute requiring the production at trial of self-incriminating documents. At first glance this case would seem to primarily involve Fifth Amendment questions. The Court, however, found that the statute requiring production of the papers was the "equivalent of a search and seizure—and an unreasonable search and seizure—within the meaning of the Fourth Amendment." [9]

The case originated when federal agents seized 35 cases of plate glass and subsequently accused E. A. Boyd and Sons of having brought the glass into the country without having paid the duty required by a customs-revenue act passed in 1874. [10] This act made failure to pay the duty an offense punishable by fine, imprisonment, and forfeiture of merchandise. [11] The statute further provided that federal judges could compel production of records. During the trial of the case in federal district court, the defendant produced invoices and other import records pertaining to the glass, in accordance with the judge's order pursuant to the statute. [12] Boyd sought to have the charge dismissed on the ground that the compulsory production of the invoices and other records violated Fourth Amendment guarantees against unreasonable searches and seizures.

Justice Bradley, writing for the Supreme Court majority, began his opinion with the concession that certain of the more aggravating elements of some search and seizure cases, such as forcible entry into a private home and a search of papers and other personal effects, were absent in this case. But, he argued, the 1874 statute did accomplish the essential object of search and seizure by forcing from a person evidence he was unwilling to give up. [13] The principal constitutional question posed was whether compulsory production of a man's private papers to be used as evidence against him in a criminal trial constituted an unreasonable search and seizure within the meaning of the Fourth Amendment. [14]

To answer this question, Justice Bradley examined the nature and scope of permissible government actions intended by the framers of the Fourth Amendment under the terms "unreasonable searches and seizures," borrowing from "the recent history of controversies on the subject, both in this country and in England." The opinion relied on the "great judgment" of Lord Camden in the English case of *Entick v. Carrington and Three Other King's Messengers,*"[15] decided in 1765. The opinion of Lord Camden in that case, "regarded as one of the permanent monuments of the British Constitution,"[16] was "in the minds of those who framed the Fourth Amendment to the Constitution, and [was] considered as sufficiently explanatory of what was meant by unreasonable searches and seizures."[17]

The *Entick* case arose when a search, conducted in the home of John Wilkes, was accompanied by the seizure of his private books and papers. The purpose of the search was to find evidence for a charge against Wilkes of seditious libel against the British government. Lord Camden viewed the search and seizure as prohibited trespass. Describing his understanding of prohibited search and seizure and the reasons for it, Lord Camden stressed that men come into political society primarily for the purpose of safeguarding their property and that, thus, the purpose of government is to safeguard private property from every improper invasion.[18] Lord Camden considered an illegal search in a private home by government to be as cruel and unjust as compulsory self-incrimination, because both invade the individual's proper sphere of privacy.[19]

Relying on the *Entick* decision, Justice Bradley reasoned that

> ...any forcible and compulsory extortion of a man's own
> testimony or of his private papers to be used as evidence
> to convict him of crime or to forfeit his goods, is within the
> condemnation of that judgment [Lord Camden's judgment].
> In this regard the Fourth and Fifth Amendments [the latter
> prohibiting compulsory self-incrimination] run almost into
> each other.[20]

Justice Bradley believed the *Boyd* case to involve not only compulsory self-incrimination but also, for reasons to be explained in a moment, illegal search and seizure: thus, he invoked the authority of English law through Lord Camden's condemnation of compulsory self-incrimination and illegal search and seizure.

The compulsory production of evidence under the 1874 statute was seen as anathema to the "pure atmosphere of political liberty and personal freedom."[21]

> [A]ny compulsory discovery by extorting the party's oath, or
> compelling the production of his private books and papers, to
> convict him of crime, or to forfeit his property, is contrary to
> the principles of a free government. It is abhorrent to the in-
> stincts of an Englishman; it is abhorrent to the instincts of an
> American."[22]

The compelled production of an invoice in opposition to the Fifth Amendment provision "that no person shall be compelled in any criminal case to
be a witness against himself,"[23] was seen by Justice Bradley as actually
constituting the illegal search and seizure. Though, Justice Bradley argued,
there was no actual search and seizure by government agents in this case,
compulsory production of the evidence accomplished for the government
the same objective as an improper or unreasonable search and seizure. He
stressed that though the government action in this case may not be as
repulsive or obnoxious as in some others, ". . . illegitimate and unconstitutional practices get their first footing . . . by silent approaches and slight
deviations from legal modes of procedure."[24]

Justice Bradley concluded his opinion by stating that the notice to Boyd
to produce the papers was unconstitutional because the judicial order and
the 1874 statute upon which that order was based violated the Fourth
Amendment. Thus, the admission of the papers into evidence at the trial
was unconstitutional—a violation of the Fourth Amendment. Here we have
the first clear statement of the exclusionary rule: When any seizure of
papers or things is unreasonable in the sense of the Fourth Amendment,
such papers and things may not be received by any federal court in evidence
against the person from whom they were seized. Justice Bradley ordered
the case remanded to District Court for a new trial where the invoices and
other papers could not be used in evidence against Boyd.

Justice Miller, concurring on the ground that compulsory production of
the evidence violates the Fifth Amendment self-incrimination privilege,
sharply opposed the Court's conclusions on the Fourth Amendment
questions presented. He conceded that the effect of the 1874 Act was to
compel self-incrimination, but insisted that it did not authorize an unreasonable search and seizure by police officers; it required only notice on a party
to the suit. Justice Miller stated that no seizure could take place under
the 1874 Act since the party was not physically compelled at any time to
give up custody of his papers. He argued that if the mere service of a
notice to produce a paper ". . . which the party can obey or not as he
chooses is a search, then a change has taken place in the meaning of words
. . . which I think was unknown at the time the Constitution was made . . . ."[25]

A notice to produce can be resisted, but an illegal search and seizure by law officers cannot. According to Justice Miller this fact constituted the distinction between search and seizure and notice and indicated that no search and seizure was involved.

It is noteworthy that in the first case in which the Court required exclusion of evidence obtained in violation of the Fourth Amendment, neither of the two opinions in the case grappled in detail with the question of why the Fourth Amendment necessitates such exclusion in the event of its violation.

For the next 27 years, the Court did not decide any important cases involving the exclusionary rule. Then, in 1914, the Court vigorously reasserted the exclusionary rule for federal courts in *Weeks v. United States*.[26] The *Weeks* case involved an indictment against the defendant on the charge of using the mails to transport tickets to be used as chances in a lottery. The defendant was arrested by a police officer while working at an express company at Union Station in Kansas City, Missouri. At the same time, other police officers were searching his house for evidence. A neighbor provided the police with a key which they used to gain entry to the house.

> They searched the defendant's room and took possession of various papers and articles found there, which were afterwards turned over to the United States Marshall. Later in the same day police officers returned with the Marshall, who thought he might find additional evidence, and, being admitted by someone in the house, probably a boarder, in response to a rap, the Marshall searched the defendant's room and carried away certain letters and envelopes . . . . Neither the Marshall nor the police had a search warrant.[27]

At Weeks' trial a number of lottery tickets and statements with reference to the lottery, both of which were first seized by the federal marshal, were introduced into evidence. Weeks' "petition for the return of his property and papers to be used at the trial"[28] was denied. The trial court admitted the evidence, convicted him on the charges, and imposed a sentence of fine and imprisonment.[29]

In reviewing that decision, the Court first sought to deal with the history and origin of the Fourth Amendment. Relying heavily on Justice Bradley's opinion in the *Boyd* case, the Court said that the Fourth Amendment had its origin in the determination of the Founding Fathers to avoid those hated and arbitrary practices concerning search and seizure (e.g., dragnet searches of private homes and general search warrants) which they had come to know both from their English and colonial experiences. "Resistance to these

practices had established the principle which was enacted into the fundamental law in the Fourth Amendment, that a man's house was his castle
and not to be invaded by any general authority to search and seize his
goods and papers."[30]

The Court held that exclusion of the evidence was required to protect
Weeks' Fourth Amendment rights: "If the letters and private documents
can thus be seized and held and used in evidence against a citizen accused
of an offense, the protection of the Fourth Amendment . . . is of no value,
and . . . might as well be stricken from the Constitution."[31] The strong
words used by Justice Day leave unexplained his conclusion that allowing
introduction of this evidence would be to neglect, if not to defy, the clear
instructions of the Constitution.[32]

Although Justice Day stated that the burden of adhering to Fourth
Amendment prohibitions against unreasonable searches and seizures is to be
laid directly on federal judges and law enforcement officers, the Court was
a long way from applying the exclusionary rule to the states. As the conclusion of the Weeks majority opinion stated:

> As to the papers and property seized by the twenty-one [local,
> non-federal] policemen [as apart from the Federal Marshall], it
> does not appear that they acted under any claim of Federal
> authority such as would make the Amendment applicable to
> such unauthorized seizures . . . . What remedies the defendant
> may have against them we need not inquire, as the Fourth Amend-
> ment is not directed to individual misconduct of such officials.
> *Its limitations reach the Federal Government and its agencies.*[33]
> (Emphasis added)

Searches and Seizures by Private Persons

Until the early 1920s, the Court had considered cases involving only official
misconduct. In 1921 the Court held, in *Burdeau v. McDowell,*[34] that evidence supplied to the federal government by private persons was not subject
to the exclusionary rule. The case involved a major oil company's turning
over to the U.S. Attorney General's office incriminating evidence taken from
its employee, McDowell, without his knowledge. The Court held that
Fourth Amendment protection applies only to governmental action, arguing
that the origin and history of the Fourth Amendment, as well as previous
cases, indicated that it was a restraint on the activities of sovereign authority.[35]
Since the record of this case clearly showed that there was no government in-
volvement in the seizure of the evidence, there was no unreasonable search
and seizure here within the scope of the Fourth Amendment. Thus, exclusion
was not required by the Court.[36]

Justice Brandeis, with Justice Holmes, in a brief but noteworthy dissenting opinion, protested against the use of the evidence on general grounds. He rejected the use, as evidence, of material seized by private individuals in circumstances which to him seemed disturbing and unacceptable. Justice Brandeis stated that it is contrary to our political system to give government officials "an exceptional position before the law." He further argued that courts should not dirty their hands with illegally obtained evidence because "... [r]espect for law will not be advanced by resort, in its enforcement, to means which shock the common man's sense of decency and fair play."[37]

The Exclusionary Rule and the States

In 1949 the Court, in *Wolf v. Colorado*,[38] heeded the arguments of those who called for flexibility at the state level by refusing to apply the *Weeks* doctrine of exclusion of evidence to the states through incorporation of the Fourth Amendment into the Fourteenth. The Court split by a five to four vote in its holding, an indication that a future change in one vote might alter the Court's position.

Wolf was a practicing physician in the state of Colorado who was convicted in a state court for conspiracy to commit abortion. Appointment books were seized from his office and were submitted as evidence at his trial.[39] The conviction was sustained by the state supreme court against claims that his rights under the Federal Constitution had been denied.

Justice Frankfurter, delivering the opinion of the Court, began by carefully delineating the substantive issue:

> The precise question for consideration is this: Does a conviction by a State court for a State offense deny "due process of law" required by the Fourteenth Amendment, solely because evidence that was admitted at the trial was obtained under circumstances which would have rendered it inadmissible in a prosecution for violation of a federal law in a court of the United States because there deemed to be an infraction of the Fourth Amendment as applied in *Weeks v. United States*, 232 U. S. 383?[40]

In answering the question posed, Justice Frankfurter first stated his understanding of the due process clause of the Fourteenth Amendment. On numerous occasions, he pointed out, the Court had rejected the incorporation theory—the notion that the Fourteenth Amendment applies the first eight amendments to the States in a wholesale fashion. Justice Frankfurter understood due process of law to convey "... neither formal nor fixed nor narrow requirements"[41]; because due process represents a

living principle and because it expresses those rights which a society regards
as fundamental at a given time. There cannot be a permanent catalogue of
what is implied by the phrase, frozen for all time. Justice Frankfurter said
that reliance on a neat formula (such as incorporation) to express what are
fundamental rights for enforcement purposes may satisfy our craving for
certainty and clarity, but it also diminishes or belittles the notion of due
process.[42]

At this point, Justice Frankfurter expressed his belief that the guarantees
of the Fourth Amendment, without reliance on specific methods of enforcement, should be applicable to the states. "The security of one's privacy
against arbitrary intrusion by the police . . ."[43] is basic in a free society, is
essential to the concept of ordered liberty, and is thus applied to the states
through the Fourteenth Amendment. On this basis, he reasoned that no
state could be permitted to affirmatively sanction unreasonable searches and
seizures. But, Justice Frankfurter insisted, saying that states may not
sanction such practices does not answer the questions of how the right is to
be enforced at the state level, how violations are to be deterred and what
remedies should be afforded if rights are interfered with. Such problems
are difficult and cannot be dealt with in a dogmatic fashion, he said.[44]

In Justice Frankfurter's opinion, the exclusionary rule is but one way of
deterring illegal police activity, a method the Court should not impose on
the states. He buttressed the argument for flexibility by showing the diversity of practice.

> As of today thirty-one states reject the *Weeks* doctrine, sixteen
> states are in agreement with it. Of ten jurisdictions within the
> United Kingdom and the British Commonwealth of Nations
> which passed on the question, none has held evidence obtained
> by an illegal search and seizure as inadmissible. The jurisdictions
> which have rejected the *Weeks* doctrine have not left the right to
> privacy without other means of protection . . . .[45]

On the basis of his understanding of the due process clause, Justice
Frankfurter argued that the Court should not condemn alternatives to the
rule which may be just as effective as the rule in dealing with police misbehavior. Further, the alternatives to the rule may have a greater chance of
success at the state or local level than at the federal level because public
opinion can be better focused on unacceptable police conduct and police
can be made more responsible to the community for their actions. The
federal arena, Justice Frankfurter argued, is too large for such a process to
take place.[46] Thus, the Court held that the Fourteenth Amendment does
not oblige the States to exclude illegally obtained evidence.[47]

Justices Murphy and Rutledge joined in a dissenting opinion calling for the application of the *Weeks* exclusionary doctrine in the *Wolf* case. While agreeing "with the Court that the Fourteenth Amendment prohibits activities which are proscribed by the search and seizure clause of the Fourth Amendment . . . ,"[48] Justice Murphy stated: "It is difficult for me to understand how the Court can go this far and yet be unwilling to take the step which can give some meaning to the pronouncements it utters."[49]

Justice Murphy rejected some possible remedies other than the exclusionary rule, which might be available to deter violations of the search and seizure clause. He rejected the possibility of criminal prosecution of the violators of the Fourth Amendment guarantee:

> Self-scrutiny is a lofty ideal, but its exaltation reaches new heights if we expect a District Attorney to prosecute himself or his associates for well-meaning violations of the search and seizure clause during a raid the District Attorney or his associates have ordered.[50]

Justice Murphy also rejected civil actions for damages against violators. Such a remedy is illusory, "if by 'remedy' we mean a positive deterrent to police and prosecutors tempted to violate the Fourth Amendment."[51] Thus, Justice Murphy was confident in stating that

> [A]lternatives are deceptive . . . . For there is but one alternative to the rule of exclusion.[52]

> The conclusion is inescapable that but one remedy exists to deter violations of the search and seizure clause. That is the rule which excludes illegally obtained evidence.[53]

Justice Murphy showed that in a few cities where police had been given extensive instruction in search and seizure, the number of violations had been reduced. He took this to mean that "this is an area in which judicial action has a positive effect . . . [and that] without judicial action, there are simply no effective sanctions presently available."[54]

The majority opinion of Justice Frankfurter in *Wolf* reflected the Court's reluctance to intervene in the administration of state criminal law in regard to illegal search and seizure. Shortly after the *Wolf* decision, this attitude was tested in *Stefanelli v. Minard*.[55] In this case, decided in 1951, police officers entered Stefanelli's home, searched the premises, and seized property used in bookmaking, which was a misdemeanor under New Jersey law. Subsequently Stefanelli was arrested, arraigned and indicted for bookmaking.

Stefanelli sought federal injunctive relief under the 1871 Civil Rights Act, seeking to prohibit the use of bookmaking evidence illegally obtained in the pending state prosecution. He relied heavily on the *Wolf* decision for the proposition that an illegal state search violates Fourteenth Amendment due process.

The Supreme Court noted that the case touched the very sensitive question of the degree to which federal courts should intrude into the administration of criminal law as it affects the prosecution of crimes at the state level.[56]   Because of the delicate balance to be preserved between federal and state powers in criminal matters, the Court, through the opinion of Justice Frankfurter, held that federal courts should refuse to overturn state criminal verdicts when evidence at state trials has been illegally secured[57]:

> If we were to sanction this intervention, we would expose
> every State criminal prosecution to insupportable disruption.
> Every question of procedural due process of law—with its far-
> flung and undefined range—would invite a flanking movement
> against the system of State courts by resort to the federal
> forum, with review if need be to this Court . . . .[58]

Thus, federal injunctive relief did not issue against the use by a state of evidence obtained by an illegal search and seizure. Basically, this case upheld the precedent established in *Wolf.*[59]

In 1952 the Court had some difficulty in applying the holdings in *Stefanelli*[60] and *Wolf.*[61] In *Rochin v. California,*[62] where the methods used to obtain evidence were thought to be so obnoxious as to offend the conscience, the High Court required exclusion at the state level.

This case involved a state court conviction of a defendant on a narcotics possession charge. The primary evidence was obtained using a stomach pump. The defendant had swallowed two tablets of morphine when confronted by the police. When police attempts to recover the evidence yielded no result, the defendant was transported to a hospital, where his stomach was pumped. The decision relied heavily on the striking facts of the case, which were described by Justice Frankfurter.

> Having "some information that [the petitioner here] was selling
> narcotics," three deputy sheriffs of the County of Los Angeles,
> on the morning of July 1, 1949, made for the two-story dwelling

house in which Rochin lived with his mother, common-law
wife, brothers and sisters. Finding the outside door open, they
entered and then forced open the door to Rochin's room on the
second floor. Inside they found petitioner sitting partly dressed
on the side of the bed, upon which his wife was lying. On a
"night stand" beside the bed the deputies spied two capsules.
When asked "Whose stuff is this?" Rochin seized the capsules
and put them in his mouth. A struggle ensued, in the course of
which the three officers "jumped upon him" and attempted to
extract the capsules. The force they applied proved unavailing
against Rochin's resistance. He was handcuffed and taken to a
hospital. At the direction of one of the officers a doctor forced
an emetic solution through a tube into Rochin's stomach against
his will. This "stomach pumping" produced vomiting. In the
vomited matter were found two capsules which proved to contain
morphine.[63]

Rochin was convicted under California law on the charge of possessing
morphine. The chief evidence against him, the two capsules, was admitted
over his objections. The conviction was affirmed by the federal court of
appeals. The Supreme Court granted certiorari primarily "because a serious
question is raised as to the limitations which the Due Process Clause of
the Fourteenth Amendment imposes on the conduct of criminal proceedings by the States."[64]

Due to the shocking nature of the search and seizure involved here,
Justice Frankfurter stated that he was obligated to modify his previous refusal to apply the exclusionary rule to the states. Although denying, as he
had in Wolf,[65] that the notion of due process and the standards of conduct
it imposed on government could be defined precisely, he did insist that the
notion of due process has some determinable meaning: an important part
of that meaning is that government cannot obtain convictions by means that
offend "a sense of justice."[66] Because "this is conduct which shocks the
conscience"[67]—the conduct being that of the government agents in this case
—the Fourth Amendment as applied to the States through the Fourteenth
required exclusion of this evidence. The holding in Rochin, in effect, was
that "ordinary" Fourth Amendment violations by the states do not require
exclusion, but "shocking" violations do. Justice Frankfurter left to future
courts the decision as to whether to be shocked.

Cooperation Between Federal and State Law Enforcement

Since the 1950s the Court has decided at least two major cases which raise
the problem of the extent to which one unit of government may turn over

illegally seized evidence to another unit. In *Rea v. United States*,[68] decided in 1956, the Court held that a federal officer who seized evidence on the basis of an invalid search warrant issued by the United States Commissioner should be enjoined from turning over such evidence to state authorities for use in a state prosecution and from testifying concerning that evidence.

The facts of the case were that petitioner, Rea, was indicted in a federal court for unlawful acquisition of marijuana on the basis of evidence seized under an invalid federal search warrant. The federal district court, on a motion by Rea, suppressed the evidence and eventually the indictment was dismissed. The evidence was suppressed (under Rule 41 of the Rules of Criminal Procedure) because the search warrant was improperly issued "in that it was insufficient on its face, no probable cause existed, and the affidavit was based on unsworn testimony."[69]

Subsequently, however, Rea was charged in a New Mexico state court with possession of marijuana in violation of state law. The case was to be based on the testimony of the federal agent as to his illegal search and on the evidence seized under the illegal federal warrant. The Supreme Court, in a 5-4 decision, decided to exclude any such testimony or evidence from the state trial. The Court, however, refused to decide this case in terms of the constitutional questions raised and thus made no decision about the Fourth and Fourteenth Amendment questions involved.[70] Justice Douglas for the Court invoked the federal courts' supervisory powers over federal law enforcement agencies and on this basis forbade the federal agent from testifying at the state trial. Justice Douglas stated that the Court was simply enforcing "the Federal Rules against those owing obedience to them."[71]

> The property seized is contraband which Congress has made subject to the orders and decrees of the courts of the United States having jurisdiction thereof . . . .[72]

In 1960, the Court once again confronted the problem of illegally seized evidence being turned over from one unit of government to another—the same type of problem confronted earlier in *Rea*.[73] In *Elkins v. United States*,[74] decided one year before the crucial Mapp case, the "silver platter" doctrine was specifically disapproved. That doctrine expresses the rule that evidence of a federal crime which state officers come upon in the course of an illegal search for a state crime may be turned over to federal authorities for use in a federal prosecution, so long as federal agents do not participate in the search but simply receive the illegal evidence on a "silver platter."

The petitioners in this case were indicted in a federal district court in
Oregon "for the offense of intercepting and divulging telephone communi-
cations and of conspiracy to do so."[75]

Before trial the petitioners made a motion

> to suppress as evidence several tape and wire recordings and a
> recording machine, which had originally been seized by state
> law enforcement officers in the home of petitioner . . . under
> circumstances which, two Oregon courts had found, had
> rendered the search and seizure unlawful.[76]

A proper warrant had been issued to seize obscene motion pictures, but
the search turned up some equipment used in wiretapping, and this equipment was seized illegally.

The Supreme Court granted certiorari in this case in order to consider
the constitutional validity of the silver platter doctrine.[77] The Court had
already decided that any participation by federal law enforcement officials
in illegal state searches and seizures would render the evidence inadmissible
in federal court[78]; but these were not the precise facts here. Rather, state
police had illegally seized evidence of a federal crime and then turned over
that evidence to federal officials.

Justice Stewart, writing for the majority, asserted that this case should
be decided by a new application of "the underlying constitutional doctrine
which *Wolf* established."[79] Justice Stewart noted that the *Wolf*[80] case
determined that Fourteenth Amendment due process prohibited illegal
searches and seizures by state as well as federal officers, although it did not
require the *exclusion* of the illegally seized evidence at the state level. The
incorporation of the unreasonable search and seizure protection into the
Fourteenth Amendment in *Wolf*, Stewart continues, marked "the removal
of the doctrinal underpinning"[81] for the admission of illegally state-seized
evidence in federal prosecutions. Thus, because the unreasonable search
and seizure clause was in effect in the states (without exclusion), and the
exclusionary rule, through *Weeks*,[82] was in effect in federal courts, the exclusion of illegally state-seized evidence in federal courts must logically
follow.

A two-fold rationale for the *Elkins*[83] decision was then advanced: first,
exclusion of evidence obtained illegally by the states is an exercise of the
Court's "supervisory power over the administration of criminal justice in
the federal courts"[84]; second, the purpose of the exclusionary rule is "to
deter-to compel respect for the constitutional guarantee in the only effectively
available way—by removing the incentive to disregard it."[85] The opinion

concluded by stating that abolition of the silver platter doctrine would encourage "proper" forms of cooperation between federal and state law enforcement officers.[86]

Justice Frankfurter, author of the *Wolf* decision, filed a lengthy dissenting opinion charging the Court with attempting to go beyond its powers by supervising search and seizure conducted by state officers and imposing standards intended for federal law enforcement upon state officials[87]:

> What the Court now decides is that these variegated judgments [the shifting views of members of the Court], these fluctuating and uncertain views of what constitutes an "unreasonable search" under the Fourth Amendment in conduct by federal officials, are to determine whether what is done by state police, wholly beyond federal supervision, violates the Due Process Clause. The observation in *Wolf v. Colorado,* reflecting as it did the fundamental protection of the Due Process Clause against "arbitrary" police conduct, and not the specific, restrictive protection of the Fourth Amendment, hardly supports that proposition or the new rule which the Court rests upon it.[88]

The Great Reversal

In 1961, *Mapp v. Ohio,*[89] a landmark 5-4 decision, partially overruled *Wolf* and applied the exclusionary rule to the states. The majority held that any evidence obtained by unconstitutional searches and seizures is inadmissible in a criminal trial in a state court. However, the Court sustained that part of *Wolf* which held that the underlying principle of the right of privacy as guaranteed by the Fourth Amendment was included in the Due Process Clause of the Fourteenth Amendment.

Miss Mapp was convicted of knowing possession of pornographic books, pictures and photographs, a violation of Ohio law.[90] The Supreme Court of Ohio, invoking *Wolf,* upheld her conviction despite the fact that it was based upon an unlawful search and seizure at her home.[91]

The facts of the case were fully laid out in the Supreme Court opinion:

> On May 23, 1957, three Cleveland police officers arrived at appellant's residence in that city pursuant to information that "a person [was] hiding out in the home, who was wanted for questioning in connection with a recent bombing and that there was a large amount of policy paraphernalia ["policy" is an illegal lottery, sometimes known as the "numbers game"] being hidden in the home." Miss Mapp and her daughter by a former

marriage lived on the top floor of the two-family dwelling.
Upon their arrival at the house, the officers knocked on the
door and demanded entrance but appellant, after telephoning
her attorney, refused to admit them without a search warrant.
They advised their headquarters of the situation and undertook
a surveillance of the house.

The officers again sought entrance some three hours later when
four or more additional officers arrived on the scene. When
Miss Mapp did not come to the door immediately, at least one
of the several doors to the house was forcibly opened and the
policemen gained admittance. Meanwhile Miss Mapp's attorney
arrived, but the officers, having secured their own entry, and
continuing in their defiance of the law, would permit him
neither to see Miss Mapp nor to enter the house. It appears
that Miss Mapp was halfway down the stairs from the upper
floor to the front door when the officers, in this highhanded
manner, broke into the hall. She demanded to see the search
warrant. A paper, claimed to be a warrant, was held up by one
of the officers. She grabbed the "warrant" and placed it in
her bosom. A struggle ensued in which the officers recovered
the piece of paper and as a result of which they handcuffed
appellant because she had been "belligerent" in resisting their
official rescue of the "warrant" from her person. Running
roughshod over appellant, a policeman "grabbed" her, "twisted
[her] hand," and she "yelled [and] pleaded with him" because
"it was hurting." Appellant, in handcuffs, was then forcibly
taken upstairs to her bedroom where the officers searched a
dresser, a chest of drawers, a closet and some suitcases. They
also looked into a photo album and through personal papers
belonging to the appellant. The search spread to the rest of
the second floor including the child's bedroom, the living room,
the kitchen and a dinette. The basement of the building and a
trunk found therein were also searched. The obscene materials
for possession of which she was ultimately convicted were dis-
covered in the course of that widespread search.[92]

At trial no warrant was produced; the State Supreme Court even doubted
that "there ever was any warrant . . . ."[93] The state court maintained
that under *Wolf v. Colorado,* the prosecution could not be prevented from
using what was admittedly unconstitutionally seized evidence.[94]
    Mr. Justice Clark wrote the opinion of the Court. He addressed himself
at once to the reasons behind the Court's turnabout. He stated that in
Wolf "the Court decided, that the *Weeks* exclusionary rule would not then

be imposed upon the States as 'an essential ingredient of the right . . .' "[95] [of] " 'privacy against arbitrary intrusion by the police.' "[96] Justice Frankfurter in his opinion in *Wolf* pointed out that a majority of the states had rejected the exclusionary rule. The Court's reasons for not applying the exclusionary rule to the states at that time were based, in part, on the number of states which had rejected the rule.[97] Justice Clark subsequently attacked ". . . the current validity of the factual grounds upon which *Wolf* was based."[98]

To open this attack, Justice Clark pointed to the instance of California as a state which had originally rejected voluntary adoption of the rule. Then, as Justice Clark indicated, California modified its policy and voluntarily adopted the rule because state authorities reached the conclusion that other remedies had failed to bring about compliance with constitutional provisions.[99] The experience of the states in the twelve ensuing years tended to show that remedies other than the rule had been unsuccessful.[100]

> While in 1949, prior to the *Wolf* case, almost two-thirds of the States were opposed to the use of the exclusionary rule, now, despite the *Wolf* case, more than half of those since passing upon it, by their own legislative or judicial decision, have wholly or partly adopted or adhered to the *Weeks* rule.[101]

He concluded that the factual considerations upon which *Wolf* was based had been undermined and could not be deemed controlling for the instant case.[102]

The Court saw the sanction of exclusion by state courts as the only possible way to insure Fourth Amendment privacy rights in the states. Only by such a method could the Court affirm its "high regard" of such an "inestimable human libert[y] "[103] among the states:

> Since the Fourth Amendment's right of privacy has been declared enforceable against the States through the Due Process Clause of the Fourteenth, it is enforceable against them by the same sanction of exclusion as is used against the Federal Government. Were it otherwise, then, just as without the *Weeks* rule the assurance against unreasonable federal searches and seizures would be "a form of words," valueless and undeserving of mention in a perpetual charter of inestimable human liberties, so too, without that rule the freedom from state invasions of privacy would be so ephemeral and so neatly severed from its conceptual nexus with the freedom from all brutish means of coercing evidence as not to merit this Court's

high regard as a freedom "implicit in the concept of ordered liberty."[104]

In concluding his opinion, Justice Clark argued, at some length, that the remedy for state violations of search and seizure rules must be the same as the federal remedy:

> The ignoble shortcut to conviction left open to the State tends to destroy the entire system of constitutional restraints on which the liberties of the people rest. Having once recognized that the right to privacy embodied in the Fourth Amendment is enforceable against the States, and that the right to be secure against rude invasions of privacy by state officers is, therefore, constitutional in origin, we can no longer permit that right to remain an empty promise. Because it is enforceable in the same manner and to like effect as other basic rights secured by the Due Process Clause, we can no longer permit it to be revocable at the whim of any police officer who, in the name of law enforcement itself, chooses to suspend its enjoyment. Our decision, founded on reason and truth, gives to the individual no more than that which the Constitution guarantees him, to the police officer no less than that to which honest law enforcement is entitled, and, to the courts, that judicial integrity so necessary in the true administration of justice.[105]

Justice Clark seems to be arguing here that the exclusionary rule is both a deterrent or sanction against unreasonable searches and seizures and a constitutional mandate intended to protect privacy, to insure that no person be convicted of a crime on the basis of an invasion of his privacy.

Finally, Justice Clark argued that imposition of the rule upon the states is supported by common sense. He argued that forbidding a federal prosecutor from introducing illegally obtained evidence, while allowing a state prosecutor "across the street" to introduce it, makes no sense. Thus, he argued, uniformity between state and federal practices in this area is the only sensible arrangement.[106]

Mr. Justice Harlan, joined by Justices Frankfurter and Whitaker, wrote a long dissenting opinion beginning with the conviction that the reversal of *Wolf* did not have to be reached in this case, that the Court "simply 'reached out' to overrule *Wolf.*"[107] He stated that the case could have been decided on the narrower question of whether a certain section of the Ohio criminal code involving possession of obscene material was constitutional.[108]

Turning to the merits of the Court's opinion, Justice Harlan attacked the

reasoning used by Justice Clark for imposing the *Weeks* exclusionary rule on
the states:

> At the heart of the majority's opinion in this case is the follow-
> ing syllogism: (1) the rule excluding in federal criminal trials
> evidence which is the product of an illegal search and seizure is
> "part and parcel" of the Fourth Amendment: (2) *Wolf* held that
> the "privacy" assured against federal action by the Fourth
> Amendment is also protected against state action by the
> Fourteenth Amendment; and (3) it is therefore "logically and
> constitutionally necessary" that the *Weeks* exclusionary rule
> should also be enforced against the States.
>
> This reasoning ultimately rests on the unsound premise that be-
> cause *Wolf* carried into the States, as part of "the concept of
> ordered liberty" embodied in the Fourteenth Amendment, the
> principle of "privacy" underlying the Fourth Amendment . . .,
> it must follow that whatever configurations of the Fourth
> Amendment have been developed in the particularizing federal
> precedents are likewise to be deemed a part of "ordered liberty,"
> and as such are enforceable against the States. For me, this does
> not follow at all.[109]

Justice Harlan argued that change in this area may take some time and
that the varying conditions of law enforcement among the states render
imposition of the uniformity sought by the majority highly inappropriate
and damaging:

> The preservation of a proper balance between state and federal
> responsibility in the administration of criminal justice demands
> patience on the part of those who might like to see things move
> faster among the States in this respect. Problems of criminal
> law enforcement vary widely from State to State. One State,
> in considering the totality of its legal picture, may conclude
> that the need for embracing the *Weeks* rule is pressing because
> other remedies are unavailable or inadequate to secure compli-
> ance with the substantive Constitutional principle involved.
> Another, though equally solicitous of Constitutional rights, may
> choose to pursue one purpose at a time, allowing all evidence
> relevant to guilt to be brought into a criminal trial, and dealing
> with Constitutional infractions by other means. Still another
> may consider the exclusionary rule too rough-and-ready a
> remedy, in that it reaches only unconstitutional intrusions which
> eventuate in criminal prosecution of the victims. Further, a

> State after experimenting with the *Weeks* rule for a time may,
> because of unsatisfactory experience with it, decide to revert
> to a non-exclusionary rule. And so on.[110]

He believed that the majority opinion would put the states in a straitjacket
and possibly cause them peculiar problems in dealing with criminal law enforcement within their borders.[111] Finally, Justice Harlan accused the
majority of using an approach ". . . which regards the issue as one of
achieving procedural symmetry or of serving administrative convenience
. . . ."[112] He claimed that the majority had misunderstood its role as
arbiter between state and federal power and had used the Fourteenth
Amendment as a vehicle for imposing on the states its own notion of
". . . how things should be done."[113]

The "Fruits" of Illegal Search and Seizure

Following *Mapp,* the Court in 1963, extended the scope of the exclusionary
rule beyond simply the material seized during an illegal search. In *Wong
Sun v. United States*[114] the Court extended the rule to include verbal
evidence which was obtained as the "fruit" of an illegal search. However,
the "taint" or "fruit of the poisonous tree" doctrine, as it came to be
called, first appeared in 1920 in *Silverthorne Lumber Co. v. United States.*[115]
In *Silverthorne,* the federal government forced compulsory production of
the corporate books and papers of the company for use in a criminal proceeding against its officers, Frederick W. Silverthorne and his father. However, the information upon which the subpeonas were based was derived
by the government from a previous unconstitutional search and seizure of
the company's offices, planned and executed by federal officers (the search
was illegal because the warrant was void).

Justice Holmes, writing for the majority, held that the government could
not use information obtained during an illegal search to subpeona the very
documents illegally viewed (in fact, copied) and then returned. He argued
that the protection of the Constitution extends not only to physical possession of the documents, but to ". . . any advantages that the Government
can gain over the object of its pursuit by doing the forbidden act."[116]
Justice Holmes justified this part of the poisonous tree doctrine by calling
it a logical extension of the fundamental notion that government should
not benefit from its own wrongdoing.[117] While supporting the general
normative idea that wrongdoers should not benefit from their wrongdoing,
Justice Holmes seems to be saying implicitly that if the government were
able to enjoy the direct or indirect fruits of its illegal activity, the deterrent
effect of the rule would be undermined.

Wong Sun v. United States[118] represented the Court's first significant excursion into the search and seizure field since the historic ruling in *Mapp v. Ohio*.[119] In *Wong Sun,* verbal evidence was held inadmissible on the ground that it derived "so immediately from an unlawful entry and an unauthorized arrest" that it was "no less the 'fruit' of official illegality than the more common tangible fruits of the unwarranted intrusion."[120]

Petitioners Wong Sun and James Wah Toy were tried and convicted in federal district court on a charge of "fraudulent and knowing transportation and concealment of illegally imported heroin."[121] The convictions were affirmed by the federal court of appeals.

The facts of this case are quite detailed but can be summarized as follows: Federal agents went to the home of James Wah Toy early one morning and, after forcing themselves illegally into the premises, obtained certain statements incriminating a certain Johnny Yee. Yee was arrested shortly thereafter in his home for possession of narcotics which he claimed to have received from Toy and Wong Sun.[122]

The crucial evidence which the government used at trial to prove the petitioner's (Wong Sun's) possession of narcotics

> consisted of four items which the trial court admitted over timely objections that they were inadmissible as "fruits" of unlawful arrests or of attendant searches: (1) the statements made orally by petitioner Toy in his bedroom at the time of his arrest; (2) the heroin surrendered to the agents by Johnny Yee; (3) petitioner Toy's pretrial unsigned statement; and (4) petitioner Wong Sun's similar statement.[123]

Justice Brennan, careful to uphold the Court's exclusion precedents, found sufficient grounds to suppress the first three items of evidence. Citing *Silverthorne,*[124] the Court held that the exclusionary rule extends to the indirect as well as direct products of illegal governmental activity.[125] Because Toy's unsigned statement was the fruit of the illegal search, and the government could not have obtained these items of evidence without the illegal search and seizure, Justice Brennan ordered these items excluded. He relied upon and quoted Justice Holmes' statement in *Silverthorne* that the government should not benefit from its own illegal acts. Thus it seems that an underlying, though unstated, rationale, here as in *Silverthorne,* is that, if the government were able to benefit, even indirectly, from its illegal acts, the deterrent objective of the exclusionary rule would be seriously compromised. Also, Justice Brennan seems to support Justice Brandeis' normative idea that wrongdoers, including the government, should not benefit from their wrongdoing.

Reasonableness in State Searches and Seizures

In *Ker v. California,*[126] the Court, in 1963, further explicated *Mapp* by addressing itself to the question of what would constitute reasonable standards for state searches and seizures and thus what evidence was subject to the exclusionary rule.

The Court ruled in *Ker*[127] that evidence obtained in an unannounced entry by state police could be used in a state court, but that minimum standards of admissibility in state courts must meet the constitutional standard prohibiting unreasonable searches and seizures, as defined in the Fourth Amendment. Although there may be more stringent federal regulations calling for suppression of illegally obtained evidence in a federal prosecution, the states must be governed by due-process standards.

The facts of the case indicate that police officers, without announcing themselves, quietly entered the Kers' apartment (in order to prevent destruction of evidence) and conducted a warrantless search yielding three packages of marijuana, which they seized. Because of the surreptitious entry gained by means of a passkey, the Kers' were caught at home with the marijuana in plain sight; they were arrested on suspicion of violating the state narcotics law. At the Kers' trial, the packages of marijuana were admitted as evidence over the petitioners' timely objections, and the Kers were subsequently convicted. A California appeals court held that there was probable cause for the arrests (because petitioners had recently purchased marijuana from a known dealer), and that since the search was incident to a lawful arrest, it was legal. Because the search was legal, the California appeals court held its fruits to be admissible.[128]

Justice Clark, writing the opinion for another 5-4 majority, took the opportunity to clarify what the Court had intended to convey in *Mapp.*[129] He stated that the rules governing admissibility of evidence in federal criminal trials are not confined to those rules derived from the Fourth Amendment; the Court has formulated additional rules of evidence for federal criminal prosecutions based on its supervisory authority over the administration of criminal justice in the federal courts. Thus, *Mapp*, as a state case, is not to be understood as establishing the Court's supervisory power over state courts and it implies ". . . no total obliteration of state laws relating to arrests and searches in favor of federal law."[130] Also, Justice Clark denied that *Mapp* lays down a "fixed formula" with regard to the reasonableness of state searches and seizures. He stressed that reasonableness remains, in the first instance, a matter for the trial court to determine.[131] At this point, Justice Clark described in detail how the Court intended to distinguish between the appropriate spheres of federal and state authority in this field and thus provided the States with some insight about how future cases arising from *Mapp* might be decided. The Supreme Court

> will, where necessary to the determination of constitutional
> rights, make an independent examination of the facts, the find-
> ings, and the record so that it can determine for itself whether
> in the decision as to reasonableness the fundamental—i.e., con-
> stitutional—criteria established by this Court have been respected.
> [However], the States are not thereby precluded from developing
> workable rules governing arrests, searches and seizures to meet
> "the practical demands of effective criminal investigation and law
> enforcement" in the States, provided that those rules do not
> violate the constitutional proscription of unreasonable searches
> and seizures and the concomitant command that evidence so
> seized is inadmissible against one who has standing to complain.[132]

The Court held that the method of entering the home in *Ker* did not "offend federal constitutional standards of reasonableness [because it was incident to a lawful arrest] and therefore [did not] vitiate the legality of an accompanying search."[133]

In 1964 the Court extended the *Ker* standard of reasonableness in a warrantless search to a search based on a warrant and thus further extended the scope of the exclusionary rule. In *Aguilar v. Texas*[134] the Court reversed a narcotics conviction where evidence was seized during a search authorized by a warrant. The Court held that the warrant issued did not meet the Fourth and Fourteenth Amendment standards of reasonableness because the magistrate issuing the warrant had insufficient information to justify approval of the warrant.

Retroactivity

In 1965, the Court, in *Linkletter v. Walker*,[135] was asked to rule on the possible retroactive application of the *Mapp* exclusionary rule upon state criminal convictions decided before 1961. Linkletter was convicted of burglary by a Louisiana court where illegally seized evidence was admitted at his trial.[136] After the *Mapp* decision in 1961 the petitioner sought to have the exclusionary rule applied to his now concluded burglary trial, with the hope of reversing his conviction. The Supreme Court granted certiorari and held 7-2 that the exclusionary rule announced in *Mapp* did not apply to state court convictions which had become final before its rendition.

Justice Clark, for the majority, argued that the basic purpose pursued by

the Court in imposing the exclusionary rule on the states would not be
served by retroactive application of *Mapp*.

> *Mapp* had as its prime purpose the enforcement of the Fourth
> Amendment through the inclusion of the exclusionary rule within
> its rights. This, it was found, was the only effective deterrent
> to lawless police action. Indeed, all of the cases since *Wolf*
> requiring the exclusion of illegal evidence have been based on
> the necessity for an effective deterrent to illegal police action
> . . . . We cannot say that this purpose would be advanced by
> making the rule retrospective. The misconduct of the police
> prior to *Mapp* has already occurred and will not be corrected
> by releasing the prisoners involved.
>
> [The purpose of Mapp] . . . will not at this late date be served
> by the wholesale release of the guilty victims.[137]

Justice Clark seems to relegate protection of privacy, the other rationale for
the rule which he had discussed in *Mapp,* to at least a secondary position.

In addition, Justice Clark noted that retroactive application of *Mapp*
would cause practical problems in the administration of justice. For example, new exclusion hearings would have to be held dealing with evidence
which, in the meantime, had been destroyed, misplaced, or had deteriorated.
Justice Clark indicated that the original trial would be impossible to re-
construct, if evidence were excluded. Witnesses who appeared at the
original trial would either not be available or might have only faint recollec-
tions of events long since past. "To thus legitimate such an extraordinary
procedural weapon that has no bearing on guilt would seriously disrupt
the administration of justice."[138] Thus the Court refused to give the *Mapp*
rule retroactive application.[139]

Civil Damages

In 1971, the Court was called upon to decide whether a violation of the
search and seizure clause of the Fourth Amendment by a federal agent, acting under color of his authority, is sufficient cause to bring an action for
civil damages. In *Bivens v. Six Unknown Named Agents of Federal Bureau
of Narcotics*[140] the Court held that Bivens was entitled to recover damages
for any injuries he might have suffered as a result of the agents' improper
actions. Although this case did not involve questions of exclusion, it is included here because it relates directly to the material on alternatives to the
rule discussed in Chapter 4.

Bivens alleged that federal narcotics agents, acting under color of federal authority, entered and searched his apartment without a warrant and arrested him on narcotics charges. Bivens brought suit in federal district court, alleging that the arrest and search were improper. In addition, he alleged that the arrest was made using unreasonable force and conducted without probable cause.

At the time of arrest, the agents had manacled the petitioner in front of his wife and children, and threatened to arrest the entire family. Shortly thereafter, Bivens was taken to a federal courthouse and subjected to a visual strip search.[141]

The petitioner "claimed to have suffered great humiliation, embarrassment, and mental suffering as a result of the agents' unlawful conduct, and sought $15,000 damages from each of them."[142] The district court dismissed the suit but the Supreme Court reversed the judgment and remanded the case to the district court. In March 1974, each of the six agents were ordered by the Federal District Court for the Eastern District of New York to pay Bivens $100.[143]

Justice Brennan stated, for the majority, that the proposition that individuals injured through Fourth Amendment violations committed by federal officials may collect damages for their injuries is hardly novel or surprising.[144] He admitted that the Fourth Amendment does not provide for such money damages explicitly, but he relied on *Bell v. Hood* for the conclusion that ". . . where legal rights have been invaded, and a federal statute provides for a general right to sue for such invasion, federal courts may use any available remedy to make good the wrong done."[145] Thus the Court held that Bivens was entitled to initiate an action based on the Fourth Amendment to recover money damages for his injuries.[146]

Chief Justice Burger wrote a lengthy dissent criticizing the exclusionary rule, argued cogently against wholesale application of the rule to the states, and discussed some alternatives to it. It is the most eloquent and comprehensive statement of opposition to the exclusionary rule to emerge from the Supreme Court. In it, the Chief Justice criticized the various theories said to justify the rule. Referring to the deterrence theory, Chief Justice Burger argued that the realities of law enforcement render a substantial deterrent effect unlikely. Further, the Chief Justice criticized the rule for its inflexibility and its failure to distinguish between petty and serious crimes. Finally, Chief Justice Burger outlined an administrative, or quasi-judicial, remedy against the government to afford the victims of illegal search and seizure compensation and restitution. This dissenting opinion goes to the heart of the problems discussed in this book and is highly relevant to the arguments made in Chapters 3 and 4. It is thus reproduced in full as an appendix.

The Exclusionary Rule in the Grand Jury

In the late 1960s and early 1970s, an important question involving the scope of the rule was making its way to the High Court, namely, the status of illegally obtained evidence in grand jury proceedings. In 1974, the Supreme Court refused in *United States v. Calandra*[147] to extend the exclusionary rule to grand jury questions based on illegally seized evidence. Some observers interpreted this move as a sign of majority antipathy toward the rule in general (in all proceedings, including trials) and thus as a possible first step in a general movement in Supreme Court jurisprudence toward abolition of the rule.

The facts of the case are quite straightforward. A federal warrant was issued authorizing a search of John Calandra's place of business in connection with an extensive investigation of suspected illegal gambling operations. It specified that the object of the search was the discovery and seizure of bookmaking and wagering paraphernalia. During an extensive four-hour search, the agents found no gambling paraphernalia, but one agent did seize a card that he had reason to believe was a loansharking record.

A special grand jury, investigating possible loansharking activities in violation of federal law, subpeonaed Calandra to question him about the evidence seized. Calandra refused to testify, invoking his Fifth Amendment privilege against self-incrimination, and successfully petitioned for a postponement of the hearings in order to prepare a motion to exclude the evidence seized in the search on Fourth Amendment grounds. A federal district court and a court of appeals upheld the exclusion of evidence that Calandra sought. The Supreme Court granted the government's request for certiorari and reversed the judgment.[148]

The six-justice majority in *Calandra,* through Mr. Justice Powell, made several points. First, the Court addressed itself to the purpose of the exclusionary rule. Citing *Linkletter*[149] the Court stated that the primary purpose of the rule is to effectuate the guarantes of the Fourth Amendment by deterring unlawful police conduct rather than to ". . . redress the injury to the privacy of the search victim."[150] Therefore, the argument for the rule would be strongest at a trial where the government's illegal activity may result in a criminal sanction being imposed on the search victim and less strong at the grand jury level where the possibility of criminal sanctions is more remote.[151] Here the Court, as it had done in *Linkletter,* places the rationale concerning protection of privacy which it had advanced in a number of cases discussed here in at least a secondary position.

Second, the Court argued that the historic and important role of the grand jury, which has traditionally been accorded wide powers, would be compromised by introducing the exclusionary rule into its proceedings: "[n]o judge presides to monitor its proceedings. It deliberates in

secret and may determine alone the course of its inquiry. The grand
jury may compel the production of evidence or the testimony of
witnesses . . . the scope of [its] inquiry is not to be limited by doubts
whether any particular individual will be properly subject to an accusation
of crime."[152]   Thus, the level of due process protection at the grand
jury level was balanced against the need for effective and expeditious law
enforcement.

Third, the Court feared that grand jury proceedings would very likely
get weighted down in suppression motions by witnesses, such motions
being only marginally related to the major objective of the grand jury. The
long delays and interruptions of grand jury proceedings would hamper the
grand jury in its attempt to do its work.[153]

Mr. Justice Brennan, writing in dissent for himself and Justices Douglas
and Marshall, stressed for the minority that the majority was, in effect,
downgrading the exclusionary rule by ignoring its "twin goals of enabling
the judiciary to avoid the taint of partnership in official lawlessness and
of assuring the people . . . that the Government would not profit from its
lawless behavior, thus minimizing the risk of seriously undermining popular
trust in Government."[154]

Habeas Corpus

In 1976, the Court decided two cases, *Stone v. Powell* and *Wolff v. Rice,*
involving the scope of relief available in federal courts to state prisoners
who claim Fourth Amendment search and seizure violations in their state
trials.[155]   Lower federal courts had ordered new trials for David Rice and
Lloyd Powell, both convicted of murder in a state court, after the highest
courts of Nebraska and California had rejected their claims of Fourth
Amendment violations. Both men claimed that the police had obtained
evidence against them in violation of the Fourth Amendment ban on unreasonable searches and seizures.

The Court held, 6-3, that even if evidence is seized in violation of the
Fourth Amendment, federal courts should not set aside state convictions
based on such evidence, unless the state has failed to provide an opportunity
for full and fair litigation of the Fourth Amendment claim.

As a result of this ruling, a state prisoner testing his conviction on Fourth
Amendment grounds would still be able to appeal through the state judicial
system to the state's highest court and finally to the U.S. Supreme Court,
which accepts only a small fraction of such cases. But this decision fore-
closes a successful appeal to a federal district judge to set aside the conviction by issuing a writ of habeas corpus (which is an order to a prison warden

to release a prisoner), unless the appellant can show that he did not receive full and fair litigation of his Fourth Amendment claim in state court.

In his rationale for this decision, Justice Powell said that the benefits of allowing federal judges to review search and seizure claims of state prisoners long after their trials are concluded are outweighed by the costs. The costs include the suppression of evidence that is "typically reliable and often the most probative information bearing on the guilt or innocence of the defendant"[156];

> Application of the rule thus deflects the truthfinding process and often frees the guilty. This disparity in particular cases between the error committed by the police officer and the windfall afforded a guilty defendant by application of the rule is contrary to the idea of proportionality that is essential to the concept of justice. Thus, although the rule is thought to deter unlawful police activity . . . if applied indiscriminately it may well have the opposite effect of generating disrespect for the law and the administration of justice.[157]

Justice Powell acknowledged that these same costs are present when a state trial judge is required by the exclusionary rule to suppress probative evidence. But he stressed that the primary reason for excluding illegal evidence from a trial—the need to teach the police a lesson and to deter future police misbehavior—does not apply to habeas corpus proceedings held many years after the misconduct by the police.

> Even if one rationally could assume that some additional incremental deterrent effect would be present in isolated cases, the resulting advance of the legitimate goal of furthering Fourth Amendment rights would be outweighed by the acknowledged costs to other values vital to a rational system of criminal justice.[158]

Justice Powell stated that the Court "adhered to the view"[159] of *Mapp* that state judges must suppress material obtained in violation of the Fourth Amendment. He stressed that continued adherence to *Mapp* is based on certain assumptions for which empirical evidence is lacking:

> Evidence obtained by police officers in violation of the Fourth Amendment is excluded at trial in the hope that the frequency of future violations will decrease. Despite the absnece of supporting empirical evidence, we have assumed that the immediate

> effect will be to discourage law enforcement officials from
> violating the Fourth Amendment by removing the incentive to
> disregard it.[160]

Certainly, the criticism of the exclusionary rule contained in this majority
opinion raises the strong possibility that the rule will be modified or
abolished in future cases.

Justice Brennan, with whom Justice Marshall joined, filed what must be
described as a furious dissent. He accused the Court of "moving in the
direction of holding that the Fourth Amendment has no substantive content
whatever."[161] His major argument, however, was that it is a matter for
Congress, not the Court, "to prescribe what federal courts are to review
state prisoners' claims of constitutional error committed by state courts."[162]

> Until this decision, our cases have never departed from the con-
> struction of the habeas statutes as embodying a congressional
> intent that, however substantive constitutional rights are delin-
> eated or expanded, these rights may be asserted as a procedural
> matter under federal habeas jurisdiction. Employing the trans-
> parent tactic that today's is a decision construing the Constitu-
> tion, the Court usurps the authority—vested by the Constitution
> in the Congress—to reassign federal judicial responsibility for
> reviewing state prisoners' claims of failure of state courts to re-
> dress violations of Fourth Amendment rights. Our jurisdiction
> is eminently unsuited for that task, and as a practical matter the
> only result of today's holding will be that denials by the state
> courts of claims by state prisoners of violations of their Fourth
> Amendment rights will go unreviewed by a federal tribunal.[163]

In his dissent, Justice White stressed his belief that the exclusionary rule
should be modified to prevent its application in cases "where the evidence
was seized by an officer acting in the good faith belief that his conduct
comported with existing law and having reasonable grounds for his belief."[164]
Justice White stressed that application of the exclusionary rule in such cases
can in no way beneficially affect the future conduct of the officer and may
in fact cause him to be recalcitrant about doing his duty.

Conclusion

This review of Supreme Court cases developing the exclusionary rule has
omitted criticism of the Court's opinions from a legal-constitutional point of
view. However, it must be noted that the explicit provisions of the Fourth

Amendment give no guidance as to how violations of its terms are to be dealt with. As Mr. Justice Black maintained, concurring in *Mapp*[165]: ". . . the Fourth Amendment does not itself contain any provision expressly precluding the use of such [illegally obtained] evidence and I am extremely doubtful that such a provision could properly be inferred from nothing more than the basic command against unreasonable searches and seizures."[166]

In this chapter we have examined the origin and step-by-step development of the exclusionary rule in the Supreme Court (see Table 1). Beginning with holdings which excluded, at the federal level, physical evidence illegally obtained by federal officers, the Court now assumes the authority to exclude the evidence and indeed the indirect "fruits" of evidence obtained illegally by any law enforcement officer of any jurisdiction at any criminal trial. Whether these developments have improved the operation of the Fourth Amendment as an element of our criminal justice system we shall examine in the next chapter.

Notes

1. *Federal Trade Commission v. American Tobacco Co.*, 264 U.S. 298 (1924); *Stanford v. Texas*, 379 U.S. 476 (1965).

2. For the cases which laid down the law described in this paragraph, see *Boyd v. United States*, 116 U.S. 616 (1886); *Trupiano v. United States*, 334 U.S. 699 (1948); *United States v. Rabinowitz*, 339 U.S. 56 (1950); *Terry v. Ohio*, 392 U.S. 1 (1968); *Peters v. New York*, 392 U.S. 40 (1968); *Sibron v. New York*, 392 U.S. 40 (1968); *Harris v. United States*, 331 U.S. 145 (1968); *Chimel v. California*, 395 U.S. 752 (1969); *United States v. Watson*, 44 L.W. 4112 (1976).

3. *Wong Sun v. United States*, 371 U.S. 471 (1963); *Chapman v. United States*, 365 U.S. 610 (1961).

4. *Warden v. Hayden*, 387 U.S. 294 (1967). The "doorway case" is *United States v. Santana*, 44 L.W. 4970 (1976).

5. *United States v. Robinson*, 414 U.S. 218 (1973) and *South Dakota v. Opperman*, 44 L.W. 5294 (1976).

6. See especially, *Harris v. United States, Trupiano v. United States* and *United States v. Rabinowitz*, footnote 2, *supra*, for cases involving "plain sight" problems.

7. *Jones v. United States*, 357 U.S. 493 (1958); *Johnson v. United States*, 333 U.S. 10 (1948).

8. *Boyd*, footnote 2, *supra*.

9. *Ibid.*, 635.

10. *Ibid.*, 617.

11. *Ibid.*

12. *Ibid.*, 618-20.

13. *Ibid.*, 622.

14. *Ibid.*

15. 19 Howell's State Trials 1029 (Michaelmas Term 1765).

16. *Boyd,* footnote 2, *supra,* 626.

17. *Ibid.*, 626-27.

18. *Ibid.*, 627.

19. *Ibid.*, 627-29.

20. *Ibid.*, 631-32.

21. *Ibid.*, 632.

22. *Ibid.*

23. *Ibid.*, 634.

24. *Ibid.*, 635.

25. *Ibid.*, 639 (Miller, J., concurring). On an issue related to that raised in *Boyd,* the Court recently held that introduction into evidence of a person's business records seized during a search by investigators of his office does not violate the Fifth Amendment's self-incrimination provision. The Court reasoned that, because the defendant took no part in the seizure and authentication of the business records, he was under no compulsion to incriminate himself. *Andresen v. Maryland,* 44 L.W. 5125 (1976).

26. 232 U.S. 383 (1914).

27. *Ibid.*, 386.

28. *Ibid.*, 388-89.

29. *Ibid.*, 389.

30. *Ibid.*, 398.

31. *Ibid.*, 393.

32. *Ibid.*, 394.

33. *Ibid.*, 398.

34. 256 U.S. 465 (1921).

35. *Ibid.*, 475.

36. *Ibid.*

37. *Ibid.*, 477 (Brandeis, J., dissenting).

38. 338 U.S. 25 (1949).

39. Lockhart, Kamisar and Choper, *The American Constitution: Cases and Materials,* 377, note b (1970).

40. *Wolf,* footnote 38, *supra,* 26.

41. *Ibid.*, 27.

42. *Ibid.*, 27-8.

43. *Ibid.*, 27.
44. *Ibid.*, 28.
45. *Ibid.*, 29-30.
46. *Ibid.*, 32-3.
47. *Ibid.*, 33.
48. *Ibid.*, 41 (Murphy, J., dissenting).
49. *Ibid.*
50. *Ibid.*, 42.
51. *Ibid.*, 42-3.
52. *Ibid.*, 41.
53. *Ibid.*, 44.
54. *Ibid.*, 46.
55. 342 U.S. 117 (1951).
56. *Ibid.*, 120.
57. *Ibid.*
58. *Ibid.*, 123.
59. Footnote 38, *supra.*
60. Footnote 55, *supra.*
61. Footnote 38, *supra.*
62. 342 U.S. 165 (1952).
63. *Ibid.*, 166.
64. *Ibid.*, 168.
65. Footnote 38, *supra.*
66. *Rochin,* footnote 62, *supra,* 173.
67. *Ibid.*, 172.
68. 350 U.S. 214 (1956).
69. *Ibid.*, 214-15.
70. *Ibid.*, 216.
71. *Ibid.*, 216-17.
72. *Ibid.*, 216.
73. Footnote 68, *supra.*
74. 364 U.S. 206 (1960).
75. *Ibid.*, 206.
76. *Ibid.*, 206-07.
77. *Ibid.*, 208.
78. *Byars v. United States,* 273 U.S. 28 (1927) and *Gambino v. United States,* 275 U.S. 310 (1927), cited in *Ibid.*, 211.
79. *Ibid.*, 213.

80. Footnote 38, *supra.*

81. *Elkins,* footnote 74, *supra,* 213.

82. Footnote 26, *supra.*

83. *Mapp v. Ohio,* 367 U.S. 643 (1961).

84. *Elkins,* footnote 74, *supra,* 216.

85. *Ibid.,* 217.

86. *Ibid.,* 221-22.

87. *Ibid.,* 238-39 (Frankfurter, J., dissenting).

88. *Ibid.,* 239. In a recent ruling, the Court modified *Elkins* to the extent
    that evidence that is illegally seized by state law enforcement officials
    and ruled inadmissible in state criminal proceedings may be used by the
    Federal Government as evidence against the owner in a *civil* tax proceed-
    ing. *United States v. Janis,* 44 L.W. 5303 (1976).

89. Footnote 83, *supra.*

90. *Ibid.,* 643.

91. *Ibid.*

92. *Ibid.,* 644-45 (brackets added).

93. *Ibid.,* 645.

94. *Ibid.*

95. *Ibid.,* 650.

96. *Ibid.*

97. *Ibid.,* 650-51.

98. *Ibid.,* 651.

99. *Ibid.*

100. *Ibid.,* 652.

101. *Ibid.,* 651; see also, Berman and Oberst, *Admissibility of Evidence Ob-
     tained by an Unconstitutional Search and Seizure,* 55 Nw. U.L. Rev. 525,
     532-33 (1960). This study indicates that at the time of *Mapp,* one-half
     of the states did not adhere to the exclusionary rule and one state,
     Maryland, retained it as to felonies.

102. *Ibid.,* 653.

103. *Ibid.,* 655.

104. *Ibid.*

105. *Ibid.,* 660.

106. *Ibid.,* 657.

107. *Ibid.,* 674 (Harlan, J., dissenting).

108. *Ibid.,* 672-73.

109. *Ibid.,* 678-79.

110. *Ibid.,* 680-81.

111. *Ibid.*, 681.
112. *Ibid.*, 682.
113. *Ibid.*
114. Footnote 3, *supra.*
115. 251 U.S. 385 (1920).
116. *Ibid.*, 391.
117. *Ibid.*, 392.
118. Footnote 3, *supra.*
119. Footnote 83, *supra.*
120. *Wong Sun,* footnote 3, *supra,* 485.
121. *Ibid.*, 473.
122. *Ibid.*, 471-79, and Broeder, *Wong Sun v. United States: A Study in Truth and Hope,* 42 Neb. L. Rev 483, 487-90 (1963).
123. *Ibid.*, 477.
124. Footnote 115, *supra.*
125. Footnote 3, *supra,* 484.
126. 374 U.S. 23 (1963).
127. *Ibid.*
128. *Ibid.*, 23-9.
129. Footnote 83, *supra.*
130. *Ker,* footnote 126, *supra,* 31.
131. *Ibid.*, 31-2.
132. *Ibid.*, 34.
133. *Ibid.*, 38.
134. 378 U.S. 108 (1964).
135. 381 U.S. 618 (1965).
136. *Ibid.*, 621.
137. *Ibid.*, 636-38.
138. *Ibid.*, 637-38.
139. *Ibid.*, 640.
140. 403 U.S. 388 (1971).
141. *Ibid.*, 389-90.
142. *Ibid.*
143. Order #228-74.
144. *Ibid.*, 395.
145. 327 U.S. 678 (1946) in *Ibid.*, 396.
146. *Ibid.*, 397.
147. 414 U.S. 338 (1974).

148. *Ibid.,* 340-42.

149. Footnote 135, *supra.*

150. *Calandra,* footnote 147, *supra,* 347.

151. *Ibid.,* 348.

152. *Ibid.,* 348.

153. *Ibid.,* 349-50.

154. *Ibid.,* 357 (Brennan, J., dissenting).

155. 44 L.W. 5313 (1976).

156. *Ibid.,* 5320.

157. *Ibid.*

158. *Ibid.,* 5321.

159. *Ibid.*

160. *Ibid.,* 5320-21.

161. *Ibid.,* 5324, footnote 1 (Brennan, J., dissenting).

162. *Ibid.,* 5333.

163. *Ibid.*

164. *Ibid.,* 5334 (White, J., dissenting).

165. Footnote 83, *supra.*

166. *Ibid.,* 661-62.

CHAPTER 3

The Exclusionary Rule As Public Policy

The justices of the United States Supreme Court have advanced two primary public policy justifications for the rule. First, it is said to deter improper police behavior because police will have no reason to gather evidence which cannot be used in a court of law.[1] Second, it is said to guarantee that, should the state invade the privacy of individuals during the course of a search and seizure, the fruits of that invasion will prove useless to the state in its prosecution (though this justification seems to have been downgraded in *Linkletter*[2] and *Calandra,*[3] discussed in the previous chapter). In other words, this second justification, which appears so strikingly in the *Mapp* decision, portrays the rule as a partial protection of the privacy of the victims of illegal searches and seizures, which is said to be guaranteed by the Fourth Amendment search and seizure clause. We will attempt to demonstrate that the rule is not an effective deterrent to police misbehavior and that attempts to justify the rule as an effective protection of privacy are unsatisfactory. In addition, a number of disadvantages of the rule not related to deterrence or privacy will be discussed.

Privacy—The Right To Be Let Alone

With respect to the justification for the rule as a protection of privacy, consider the following two situations: First, assume that the person whose privacy is invaded is innocent of the alleged crime (or some other crime); and second, assume that he is guilty.[4] If he is innocent, the rule offers him little help, remedy or protection—and no compensation,[5] for the police will rarely find any excludable evidence and almost never find excludable evidence sufficient to convict a suspect. In a sense, the illegal search or seizure may benefit the victim by indicating his innocence, at least to the police or prosecutor.

If the suspect on whom an illegal search and seizure has been conducted is in fact in possession of incriminating evidence which is used to convict him, then we must ask whether his privacy has been invaded. To frame the question more precisely, we must ask whether evidence or information concerning a crime is of a public or of a private nature. If it is essentially a public concern, then, as I shall shortly argue, it is inappropriate to contend that the state has no right to it.

Why is information and evidence concerning a crime more of public than private concern? A certain portion of the criminal act is private—that part which concerns the perpetrator; his motivations, feelings, and in a certain sense the physical act itself. His perception and understanding of the act, its history, and its consequences to him are clearly his private, singular possession. Publicly admitting that he has committed a criminal act is often painful. But this must be balanced against the pain, harm, and difficulty caused the victim of the crime; this is clearly private to the victim, not to the perpetrator. These two considerations seem essentially to cancel each other out. What swings the balance in favor of calling the matter more public than private is society's concern that each criminal act is in violation of the established public order, and if the perpetrator goes unpunished or unrehabilitated, he may repeat his crime. In addition, if he could commit his crime with impunity, that fact might encourage others to criminal activity.[6]

If criminal activity is predominantly a public concern, then when the police, either legally or illegally, find evidence of such activity, it is not an invasion of the individual's privacy to use what the police have found against him in a criminal proceeding. Specifically, since criminal activity is not private, a location is not private if activities of great public interest—crimes —are committed or concealed there; thus, the police cannot be denied access to the location of a crime on the ground of protection of privacy. A policeman who illegally came upon a murder, robbery, assault, or drug factory, can not realistically be said to have happened upon a private act or a location which should be off limits to the police because it is regarded as private.[7] The legitimate public concern for criminal activity and, in short, the public nature of contraband, renders the search for and the seizure of that contraband (but that only) a necessary and justifiable police activity on behalf of the public. This argument for the admissibility of criminal evidence does not, of course, extend to the fruits of police action which are unrelated to search and seizure. But a legislature, by criminalizing a particular activity, indicates that the legislature regards that activity as having a significant public dimension; if this were not the case, why should public money be spent in dealing with persons who commit the designated crime?

This is not to argue that illegal police searches should not be deterred as effectively as possible. It *is* to say that when the deterrent breaks down, when the police illegally uncover a crime, murder, rape, drugs, guns, etc.— the evidence they find should be admissible in a court of law.

Furthermore, this argument justifies only the search for, seizure, and use of in court criminal evidence. It does not legitimate the use of excessive physical force by police officers or unnecessary damage to the personal property of the victim or of another person. Disciplinary action against a misbehaving officer is not limited or discouraged, as his search and seizure would be improper regardless of the guilt or innocence of the person searched. The officer commits an illegal search when he violates the rules governing proper searches and seizures (for example, by failing to obtain a search warrant) and because he cannot know whether the suspect is guilty or innocent. Finally, nothing said here limits financial compensation to the innocent victims of illegal searches and seizures for invasion of privacy. However, the guilty victim, the person with whom incriminating evidence is found, should have no such right of recovery, since, as argued above, his right of privacy has not been invaded by the search and seizure. The issue raised in this section will be dealt with again in Chapter 4.

Justice Bradley, in his majority decision in the landmark *Boyd*[8] case, asserts that the essence of what is offensive about an illegal search and seizure is the invasion by the authorities of the individual's security and liberty—what is called his right of privacy. But if, as has been argued, crime is more a public than a private matter, then it is decidedly not an invasion of the individual's legitimate privacy for the public's agents, the police, to use their discovery of criminal activity and the fruits of their investigation in court. In short, there can be no basic right of privacy for an activity which, on balance, is simply not private. Surely there are many areas of human endeavor in which the individual has a great interest in privacy, and with which, it could be argued, the state ought to have little or no concern of a legal nature. However, since crime, for the reasons given above, is not one of these, we are obligated to seriously question Justice Bradley's objection, on the ground of protection of privacy, with respect to the courtroom use of improperly obtained criminal evidence.

In sum, the argument that the exclusionary rule provides appropriate protection for both innocent and guilty victims of illegal searches and seizures is misguided. The rule is of very little help to the innocent victims of illegal searches and seizures. Also, it represents an improper and unacceptable protection of privacy for those from whom incriminating evidence has been seized, even if that evidence has been seized in an illegal manner.

Justice Clark, as well as others, argues in his majority opinion in *Mapp* that the exclusionary rule is a constitutional mandate intended to protect privacy, insuring that no person be convicted of a crime on the basis of an invasion of his privacy. But since, as argued here, illegal searches and seizures do not, as such, invade privacy, Justice Clark's argument seems misguided: If privacy is not invaded, then no constitutional mandate is needed to protect against such invasions. As to whether the rule is constitutionally mandated, it should be further noted that, while the Fourth Amendment to the Constitution does say that the right against unreasonable searches and seizures "shall not be violated," the amendment is absolutely silent as to what remedies should be available for those whose Fourth Amendment rights have been abridged. For 150 years, until 1961, the prevailing understanding on the Court was that exclusion was not required, at least at the state level; the decision imposing exclusion on the states was 5-4. These facts indicate that the "constitutional mandate" imposing exclusion on the states is a subject about which reasonable, thoughtful, and informed men can and do disagree.

Deterrence

In his study of the American exclusionary rule and the promise of the Canadian tort alternative, James Spiotto notes that an "empirical study indicated that over a 20-year period in Chicago, the proportional number of motions to suppress evidence allegedly obtained illegally increased significantly. This is the opposite result of what would be expected if the rule had been efficacious in deterring police misconduct."[9] Spiotto indicates that this increase in the number of suppression motions cannot be attributed solely to frivolous motions. In Table 1, Spiotto compares three studies conducted between 1950 and 1971 and notes a substantial increase in motions to suppress in narcotics and gun offenses and a sharp decrease in these motions in gambling cases.[10] He explains the decrease in motions to suppress in gambling cases by noting that federal prosecution of gambling offenses began during this period, taking the pressure off local police to be active in this area of law enforcement. Spiotto's conclusion is that "had the exclusionary rule deterred police from making illegal searches and seizures, one might expect the number of motions to suppress to have declined in all offenses, not just in gambling. The data demonstrate

Table 1 Motions to Suppress—1950-1971

Gambling, Weapons, and Narcotics Cases in
Branch 27 of the Municipal Court of Chicago, 1950

Offense	No. of defs.[a]	Defs. with motion to suppress (a)	Motions granted (b)	Defs. with motions granted (a) × (b)
All gambling offenses	5,848	77%	99%	76%
Narcotics	288	19	100	19
Carrying concealed weapons	513	28	91	25
All above offenses	6,649	70	98	69

Source: Comment, Search and Seizure in Illinois: Enforcement of the Constitutional Right of Privacy, 47 Nw.U.L.Rev. 493, 498 (1952).

Gambling, Weapons, and Narcotics Cases in Branches 27 and 57
of the Circuit Court in Chicago for 12 Sample Days in 1969

Offense	No. of defs.[a]	Defs. with motion to suppress (a)	Motions granted (b)	Defs. with motions granted (a) × (b)
All gambling offenses	312	52%	86%	45%
Narcotics	457	34	97	33
Carrying concealed weapons	188	36	68	24
All above offenses	957	40	87	35

Source: Dallin H. Oaks, Studying the Exclusionary Rule in Search and Seizure, 37 U. Chi. L. Rev. 665, 685 (1970).

Gambling, Weapons, and Narcotics Cases in Branches 25, 27, and 57 of
the Circuit Court in Chicago for 3 Months (April, May, June) in 1971

Offense	No. of defs.[a]	Defs. with motion to suppress (a)	Motions granted (b)	Defs. with motions granted (a) × (b)
All gambling offenses	824	32%	76%	24%
Narcotics	2,060	43	84	36
Carrying concealed weapons	929	36	62	22
All above offenses	3,813	39[b]	77	30

Source: Compiled from examination of court records in Branches 25, 27, and 57 of the First District of the Municipal Department of the Circuit Court of Cook County for April, May, June of 1971.

[a]"No. of defs." means number of defendants disposed of during the period, and does not include those whose cases were continued. For example, the total number of defendants in narcotics cases during April-May-June, 1971 would be 10,369 while the number of dispositions was 2,060.

[b]The number of motions to suppress during April-May-June, 1971 was as follows: Narcotics—878; Guns—335; Gambling—255; and other felony offenses—84.

otherwise." One might argue that the increase in the number of motions to suppress was due to an increased number of unmeritorious motions. For example, Spiotto notes, during the 21 year period motions to suppress in narcotics offenses increased 24% while motions granted decreased by 16%. But Spiotto argues that "since the decrease in the number of motions to suppress granted does not equal the increased number of motions in narcotics cases, the rise in motions over a 21 year period cannot be attributed solely to their frivolous nature. Gun cases also reflect this phenomenon."[11] Spiotto concludes from his study:

> The empirical study demonstrates not only the inequities of the exclusionary rule but also the fact that the deterrent rationale for the rule does not seem to be justified . . . The increasing dissatisfaction of eminent jurists and legal scholars cannot go unheeded. Thus, given the present status of the law and the workings of the exclusionary rule, change is warranted . . . .[12]

One of the most comprehensive studies of the exclusionary rule ever undertaken is that of Dallin Oaks.[13] He reviews the history and suggested justifications for the rule, presents empirical evidence on the effect of the rule on police searches and seizures, discusses the problem of deterrence and applies it to the exclusionary rule, analyzes the limitations upon the deterrent effectiveness of the rule in certain circumstances, and discusses a number of negative effects of the rule. Oaks states in this study of the operation of the rule that ". . . the figures [for motions to suppress] at least show that the exclusionary rule has not been effective in persuading the Chicago police to observe the search and seizure rules in anywhere near as high a proportion of cases as they are able."[14] Further, Oaks' study of law enforcement in Cincinnati between 1956 and 1967 indicates that the Supreme Court's imposition of the exclusionary rule on the states had no significant effect on the number of arrests or convictions in Cincinnati in narcotics, weapons or gambling cases. This fact, according to Oaks, indicates that imposition of the rule did not have a significant effect on Cincinnati police search and seizure practices in these kinds of cases.[15] Figures 1 and 2 illustrate Oaks' data.[16] Near the end of his study, Oaks argues:

> As a device for directly deterring illegal searches and seizures by the police, the exclusionary rule is a failure. There is no reason to expect the rule to have any direct effect on the overwhelming majority of police conduct that is not meant to result in prosecutions, and there is hardly any evidence that the rule exerts

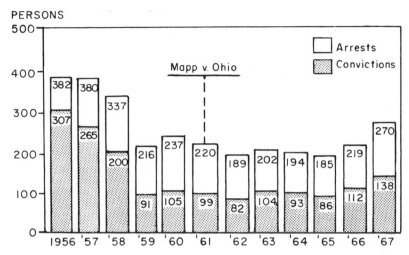

Figure 1 Weapons arrests and convictions by Cincinnati police, 1956 to 1967. Weapons offenses include carrying and possession. In this and the next figure arrests equal total persons charged by police plus persons released by police without formal charges. Convictions are persons found or pleaded guilty, whether arrested in that year or the previous one.

Source: Cincinnati Police, Annual Report of the Division of Police, 1956 through 1967, Table 24.

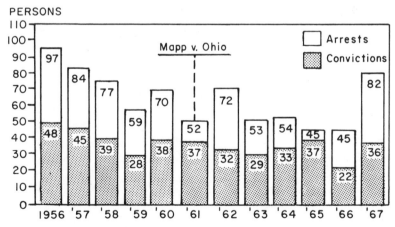

Figure 2 Narcotics arrests and convictions by Cincinnati police, 1956 to 1967.

Source: Same as Figure 1.

any deterrent effect on the small fraction of law enforcement
activity that is aimed at prosecution. What is known about the
deterrent effect of sanctions suggests that the exclusionary rule
operates under conditions that are extremely unfavorable for
deterring the police. The harshest criticism of the rule is that
it is ineffective. It is the sole means of enforcing the essential
guarantees of freedom from unreasonable arrests and searches
and seizures by law enforcement officers, and it is a failure in
that vital task.[17]

Michael Ban's two studies of the impact of the rule in Boston and
Cincinnati,[18] conducted in the mid-1960s, tend to confirm the ineffectiveness of the rule. Table 2 summarizes his data. Believing these data to be
reasonable indicators of the degree to which the police were complying
with *Mapp,* Ban concludes that the rule showed spotty effectiveness in
Boston and almost none in Cincinnati. Ban attributes the low number of
motions to suppress—both made and granted—not to the effectiveness of
Mapp, but to ignorance by lawyers and defiance by judges of that decision.
Ban speculates that the rule will have some effect in some jurisdictions, but
he concludes, in general, that the rule is not an effective deterrent
instrument.

A recent study by Bradley C. Canon,[19] however, suggests that the conclusions of Oaks and others about the deterrent value of the rule are too
harsh. Canon criticizes the probative value of earlier studies, but each of
his criticisms seems to be flawed. Canon first argues that evidence and data
gathered in studies previous to his are inconclusive because they are drawn
from an insufficient sample.[20] Yet, Canon admits that substantial data were
gathered for the previous studies from at least five major American cities—

Table 2 Summary of Ban's Data*

Data	Before *Mapp* (1960)	After *Mapp* (1963)
Search warrants issued in Boston	About 100	Nearly 1,000
Search warrants issued in Cincinnati	Virtually 0	About 100
Motions to suppress in Boston	0	Over 100 (25% granted)
Motions to suppress in Cincinnati	0	Around 35 (40% granted)

*All figures are per year. Both Boston and Cincinnati did not exclude illegally ob-
tained evidence prior to *Mapp.*

Cincinnati, Boston, Washington, D.C., Chicago and New York—and further admits that it would be fair to treat these studies as an indictment of the rule, if not a conviction.[21] Second, Canon argues that much of the evidence condemning the rule is dated.[22] But he admits that there are "compelling reasons" for this, namely, the value of comparing data from the periods before and after the crucial *Mapp* decision of 1961.[23] Furthermore, the evidence gathered by Spiotto showing the ineffectiveness of the rule in Chicago over a long period of time, from 1950 to 1971, is not significantly dated. Finally, Canon argues that the perspective of previous studies was to seek out "evidence of the rule's failure or upon finding it they have spotlighted it in their discussions," and that "nobody has searched for evidence or illustrations of compliance with the Fourth Amendment."[24] But Canon fails to bring forward any evidence of bias in the previous studies and he does not call into question either the data or the inferences from the data for the jurisdictions and time periods under scrutiny in the previous studies.

Canon then describes the findings of his own empirical research into the effectiveness of the rule in large American cities. He considers four types of data: The effect of the rule on (1) the number of arrests for crimes most likely to involve search and seizure, such as narcotics, weapons and gambling offenses; (2) the number of search warrants issued; (3) changes in police search and seizure policies, and (4) the number of successful motions to suppress evidence or of dismissals of charges.[25] Canon's conclusions from this research indicate that the rule is more effective than Spiotto, Oaks, and Ban have concluded, but his data do not show that the rule has accomplished the tasks for which it was designed:

> For those seeking conclusive evidence about the efficacy of the exclusionary rule, the findings reported above are probably disappointing. Different measures point in varied and sometimes slightly contradictory directions and some of the results are subject to ambiguous interpretation. Taken as a whole, the main emphasis to be put on the findings is a negative one: they cast considerable doubt on earlier conclusions that the rule is ineffective in deterring illegal police searches . . . [T]here are still circumstances in which the rule has a minimal impact on police behavior. But these circumstances are comparatively few. Most of our data do not permit such an inference. Indeed, a good many of the findings support a positive inference—that the rule goes far toward fulfilling its purpose. Beyond this, the incomplete nature of the data and the ambiguity of its interpretation serve to aid arguments on behalf of the rule's effectiveness

because in this situation at least it is easier to demonstrate the
existence of widespread non-compliance with the fourth amendment than it is to demonstrate compliance. It is usually
necessary to support assertions of compliance by inference
rather than direct evidence; and such inferences are always subject to a counter-argument that one is not using the right
measure or looking in the right places. Nonetheless, the in-
conclusiveness of our findings is real enough; they do not nail
down an argument that the exclusionary rule has accomplished
its task.[26]

There can be no doubt that a certain number of illegal acts are deterred
by the rule, for many law officials must be reluctant to gather evidence
which will be of no value in court. However, there are several reasons for
doubting the effectiveness of the rule as a deterrent.

First, the operating scope of the rule is limited to exclude only that
evidence presented at trial. The trial constitutes a narrow stage in the criminal process, especially considering the amount of plea bargaining taking
place today, and the trial affects a small proportion of police activity. As
the President's Commission on Law Enforcement and the Administration of
Justice pointed out, "A great majority of the situations in which policemen
intervene are not, or are not interpreted by the police to be, criminal situations in the sense that they call for arrest with its possible consequences
of prosecution, trial and punishment."[27] Because the rule affects prosecution and conviction, it provides no remedy for police practices not aimed at
them, but rather at harassment or seizure of contraband. Thus, blatant misbehavior by police such as physical abuse, illegal detentions or various ex-
tortion schemes that do not aim at prosecution and conviction are unaffected
by the rule because they remain outside its scope. Although police officers
may be prosecuted for such misbehavior, such prosecution is at the discretion of the prosecutor. As will be discussed in Chapter 4, the prosecutor
generally requires a good relationship with the police to carry out his duties
effectively and, thus, cannot be relied upon to prosecute cases involving
police misbehavior. The substantial difficulties with current civil actions
against the police will also be discussed in Chapter 4.

Studies by both Lafave and Miller indicate that there are certain kinds of
criminal activity in response to which police have generally emphasized unlawful harassment, agitation, and seizure of contraband rather than prosecution and conviction.[28] These types of criminal activity tend to be the
so-called victimless crimes such as gambling, liquor and narcotics violations,
and prostitution. Improper, illegal and often abusive searches and seizures
for evidence of these crimes are substantially unaffected by the exclusionary

rule because of the tendency not to prosecute in these areas. Indeed, a
recent study indicates that the *Mapp* decision has increased the use of
illegal patrol techniques, including unlawful searches and seizures, because
of police fear that exclusion of evidence mandated by *Mapp* would prevent
successful prosecution.[29]

In addition to evidence that the rule has little or no deterrent effect on
many kinds of police misbehavior, there are even some strong indications,
as noted above, that it encourages certain kinds of police misconduct.
There is evidence that policemen rely on departmental standards for justification of their actions more than legal standards of behavior.[30] In relation
to the exclusionary rule, this finding indicates that when a policeman's
fellow officers and superiors place a very high priority on convicting a
suspect, and when perjury by the policeman is necessary to prevent exclusion of evidence at trial, the policeman may risk perjury to convict the
suspect and thus conform to departmental norms. Indeed, the evidence
which exists on this subject strongly indicates that such false testimony is
being given by police.[31] Second, the rule encourages or at least allows,
official misconduct of another kind: Police purposely obtaining evidence
illegally against suspects whom they wish, for any number of reasons, to
have set free. For example, one study dealing with this problem notes that
the same police officers are involved repeatedly in illegally conducted
gambling raids which could very easily have been carried out in a legal manner, for example, by obtaining arrest warrants. The study concludes that
some gambling raids are intentionally conducted in violation of search and
seizure rules ". . . to immunize the gamblers while at the same time satisfy-
ing the public that gamblers are being harassed by the police."[32] Thus, the
exclusionary rule provides virtually undetectable possibilities for the police
to engage in corruption.

If one examines the effects of the rule, it is clear that its impact falls
only indirectly on the policeman. It is no direct punishment of the errant
officer. As Justice Jackson wrote: "Rejection of [the] evidence does
nothing to punish the wrongdoing officials . . ."[33] Suppression does not
affect his official status as a policeman; he is not censured by his fellow
officers or the Court. It simply lets the criminal go free. In addition, as
will be discussed later, disciplinary action is rarely taken directly against
the officers specifically responsible for the exclusion of certain evidence.
Although it may be unpleasant for a police officer to have a case on which
he has worked (perhaps long and hard) dismissed because of improper activity by him or by his colleagues, the rule does not affect his pay, his job
security, or his tenure; nor does it even insure that he will be disciplined in

any way for illegal behavior. Chief Justice Burger notes that law enforcement agencies generally do not impose direct discipline on the individual
officer responsible for a particular application of the rule.[34] Oaks stresses
that police discipline is not imposed upon officers whose searches and
seizures are judged illegal at trial.[35] Thus, there is little done to the
offending officer to change his practices. This fact constitutes a crucial
deficiency in the rule.

It is the opinion of Fred E. Inbau and others that the policeman who is
inclined to ignore legal guidelines will not be deterred from acting in an
illegal way in order to obtain evidence merely because the evidence he ob-
tains would be inadmissible in court.

Inbau believes that although a trial judge or a prosecutor might be sufficiently "sensitive" to the possibility of reversal on these grounds, this type
of reaction from a police officer is highly unlikely. He contends that the
"ordinary" policeman is far too untrained and insensitive to be sufficiently
impressed by these methods of deterrence:

> They are generally insensitive to a court's rejection of evidence
> merely because of the impropriety of the methods used to ob-
> tain it. Moreover, the most insensitive of all is the ignorant,
> untrained policeman—the one whose improper practices are most
> disturbing . . . it is almost futile to try to improve police
> practices by rejecting improperly obtained evidence of guilt.
> The courts may just as well attempt to solve the problems of
> juvenile delinquency by giving courtroom reprimands to the
> parents of delinquents.[36]

Inbau goes on to assert that the incidence of police misconduct is in-
versely proportional to the extent to which policemen are qualified and
trained. Therefore, the problem cannot be solved through mere exclusion
of evidence. Its solution requires a general upgrading in the choice and
training of police officers.

In addition to the above, there are many important factors which limit
the impact of the rule on police behavior. Officers whose illegal actions
result in loss of convictions may still receive the implicit or explicit
approval of their superiors if their behavior conforms to police group
norms.[37] Also, police and courts take different views of the role of the
police officer: "The individualistic, rule-oriented perspective of the courtroom is at variance with the situational, order maintenance perspective of
the patrolman."[38] Thus, even if an officer's evidence is suppressed in
court, he may understand that he has done his duty by confiscating it;

indeed, judges seem to have been less than successful in convincing police otherwise, as indicated by the great number of illegal searches and seizures. Trial judges often do not explain clearly to officers why their evidence is being excluded, nor do they suggest to the officer how such mistakes may be avoided in the future. Thus, the impact of the rule must be greatly limited if police are not even informed of the nature of their wrongdoing.[39] Indeed, Oaks personally observed policemen leaving courtrooms bitter and confused about exclusion of evidence.[40] Given the large number of defendants who either plead guilty to the original charge or plead guilty to a lesser offense as a result of plea bargaining, the instances in which the rule can be applied are greatly reduced. "Why should court exclusion of evidence or appellate reversal of trial decisions deter police when ninety percent of the time there will be no trial?"[41] However, loss of convictions through exclusion of evidence is not as serious a matter for the police officer as might be thought. Police effectiveness (and thus promotion, salary, etc.) is judged by the number of arrests which "solve" crimes as far as police are concerned, and not by the number of convictions. Lastly, in those jurisdictions where prosecutors decline to prosecute cases with severe search and seizure problems, there are relatively few instances in which the rule can be invoked. Thus the impact of the rule can become quite indirect, if not almost entirely eliminated.[42]

The real brunt of the exclusionary rule's effect is actually borne by the prosecution, which has virtually no power to prevent or punish police misconduct:

> the immediate impact of the exclusionary rule falls not upon the police but upon the prosecutor who is attempting to obtain a conviction. The impact is misplaced. The Presidential Commission's Report on the Police observed that the prosecutor is not generally conceived of in this country as having overall responsibility for the supervision of the police. The relationship is generally that of independent and coordinate authorities, not always cooperating and sometimes even in conflict in the common task. The relationship can be explained in terms of the different motivations of prosecutor and police. The prosecutor's dominant career motivation is to prosecute and convict the guilty. The police, on the other hand, have a variety of motives other than to facilitate prosecutions. Consequently, the exclusionary rule is well tailored to deter the *prosecutor*. But the prosecutor is not the guilty party in an illegal arrest or search and seizure, and he rarely has any measure of control over the police who are responsible.[43]

The two major legal rationales supporting the rule, as can be seen from the Supreme Court decisions reviewed in Chapter II, are deterrence of improper law enforcement practices and protection of privacy. As Justice Clark said concerning privacy in *Mapp*," [the Fourth Amendment's right of privacy] is enforceable against the states . . . by the same sanction of exclusion as is used against the Federal Government."[44]   And as Justice Murphy said concerning deterrence in *Wolf*, "The conclusion is inescapable that but one remedy exists to deter violations of the search and seizure clause. That is the rule which excludes illegally obtained evidence."[45]   This chapter has attempted to demonstrate that the rule has been a failure on both of these counts.

Because the rule does not aid, compensate, or protect innocent victims after illegal invasions of their privacy, and because, as argued earlier, it affords unjustified and improper protection of privacy for the guilty victims of illegal searches and seizures, the rule cannot be seen as a proper protection of privacy for innocent or guilty victims of illegal searches and seizures, *except* insofar as it acts as a deterrent against future illegal searches and seizures—and there are serious reasons to doubt the deterrent effect of the rule. Thus, the two major arguments (deterrence and protection of privacy) made by proponents of the rule do not provide a satisfactory justification for its existence.

Justice Brandeis argued that respect for law and the courts would not be advanced if the courts sullied their hands by allowing illegally obtained evidence to be admitted.[46]   Justice Holmes' argument that courts should not tolerate government (as the people's agent) benefiting directly or indirectly from its wrongdoing is related to the above argument because it involves the morality of government activity.[47]   Both of these arguments are derived from the provisions in the Fifth and Fourteenth Amendments (applying to the federal government and the states, respectively) that life, liberty, or property shall not be taken without due process of law. We will indicate in this chapter that the exclusionary rule brings the law and the court system into disrepute, but we shall discuss the aforementioned "propriety" arguments and the reply to them more fully in the next chapter. The reply to these arguments is given there because the reader must be familiar with the alternative to the exclusionary rule proposed in Chapter 4 in order to understand that reply.

Other Disadvantages of the Rule

Turning away from the deterrence problem and toward other disadvantages of the rule, another serious difficulty with the rule is that a certain number of guilty persons escape conviction because of its operation. Indeed, Oaks' study of motions to suppress in gambling, narcotics, and weapons cases in Chicago indicates that "in every single one of these cases in which a motion to suppress was granted, the charges were then dismissed." Oaks concludes that these proceedings focus almost entirely on evidentiary questions, rather than on the guilt or innocence of the suspect.[48] It is sometimes possible to retry a suspect on the basis of evidence other than that illegally obtained; often, however, it is not, and persons dangerous to society are released. Virgil Peterson has made this point well, and has related it to the peculiar ineffectiveness of the rule in protecting the innocent:

> Rejection of the evidence does nothing to punish the wrong-doing official, while it may, and likely will, release the wrong-doing defendant. It deprives society of its remedy against one lawbreaker because he has been pursued by another. It protects one against whom incriminating evidence is discovered, but does nothing to protect innocent persons who are the victims of illegal but fruitless searches. The disciplinary or educational effect of the court's releasing the defendant for police misbehavior is so indirect as to be no more than a mild deterrent at best.[49]

Related to this point is another important difficulty with the rule: it undermines public respect for the legal and judicial system. One complaint about the legal system is that too many suspects are released on technicalities. In fact, this complaint most often refers to the operation of the exclusionary rule. Thus, far from increasing public respect for the court system in the public mind, the operation of the rule may cause that system to appear dangerously foolish, not only to the disgruntled police officers directly affected by it, but to large segments of the public. Indeed, the public expects from its courts both adherence to certain standards of due process and conviction of the guilty (and thus acquittal of the innocent); under the operation of the exclusionary rule, it gets the former but in many cases not the latter.[50]

Another difficulty with the rule as it has been applied to the states in accordance with *Mapp*,[51] is that it fails to distinguish between more and less serious offenses. Both a gambler and a murderer, having committed crimes of widely differing degrees of gravity, would be given reversals of their convictions because of the illegality of a search and seizure. The operation of the rule frees the criminal without giving any consideration to the danger to which society is exposed by this release.[52] But the law is accustomed to taking into account the seriousness of the alleged crime, even before the trial is completed and sentence is pronounced. Whether a person may be released at all in the pretrial period and the amount of bail, if he is released, are determined in part by the seriousness of the crime allegedly committed (though bail is also determined by the probability of the defendent's appearing for trial). Thus, there is precedent for applying different standards to crimes of differing degrees of gravity.

Also, as noted earlier, the rule does not distinguish between a willful and flagrant violation by an officer, and an exercise, under strained circumstances, of his best judgment, a judgment which, only after several appeals, may be held by a perhaps divided appellate court to have been improper. The issues which appellate decisions resolve are both controversial and difficult, as evidenced by courts sharply divided on the issue of what is a reasonable search and seizure. After all, if appellate judges are not sure about the legality of an officer's action after long consideration of a written record, it is asking a great deal of the officer that he judge the matter correctly in a few moments. Nor can judges be oblivious to the fact that their opinions sometimes lack that kind of helpful guidance which will aid a law enforcement officer in the actual performance of his duty. Police officers should not be deterred from exercising "reasonable judgment," though that judgment may not represent the final judgment of the appellate courts as to proper behavior in that situation.[53] In the same vein, the rule does not distinguish harmless errors of judgment which work no serious injustice and which do not seriously deprive the suspect of his rights, from the flagrant violations of the Fourth Amendment such as those seen in *Mapp*[54] or *Rochin*[55] which result in serious deprivations of rights. As Chief Justice Burger says in *Bivens*: ". . . society has a right to expect rationally graded responses to police misconduct—depending on its seriousness—rather than the universal 'capital punishment' we inflict on any and all evidence when police error is shown in its acquisition.[56]

Another problem with the rule is that it often excludes the most credible kinds of evidence. Thus, it is erroneous to link "legal" evidence with the best, most credible kinds of evidence; for evidence that is seized, perhaps illegally, in a "state of nature" has most often not been "prepared" by anyone for presentation as evidence in a court of law and thus, ironically, though it is presently inadmissible because illegally obtained, may be the most credible evidence available to aid in a proper and just dispostion of cases. Thus, application of the exclusionary rule on search and seizure grounds is qualitatively different from other types of exclusion such as suppression of unreliable confessions, line-up evidence, or eyewitness identification, for in these other areas suppression takes place because of specific doubts as to the reliability of the evidence. In search and seizure, the probative value of physical evidence, while hardly in doubt, is often ignored.[57]

Finally, application of the rule has two clearly harmful side effects. First, the rule intensifies plea bargaining because prosecutors who fear suppression of important evidence at trial, may be willing to negotiate regarding the seriousness of the charge or sentencing recommendations rather than risk dismissal.[58] In addition, a number of commentators have pointed out that the necessity of excluding obviously probative evidence under the rule has placed increasing pressure on judges to sanction dubious searches and seizures based on dangerously expanded notions of probable cause. Judges feel they must interpret probable cause expansively in order to admit crucial evidence. Thus, the exclusionary rule may have the perverse and unintended effect of limiting the scope of privacy contemplated by the Fourth Amendment.[59]

Conclusion

The preceding represents the major outline of the indictment to be made against the exclusionary rule and its present operation. We have argued that the public policy justifications advanced for the rule, protection of privacy and deterrence of illegal police misbehavior, are inadequate. We have discussed important liabilities of the rule not related to privacy or deterrence: its effect of releasing otherwise guilty persons, its tendency to undermine public respect for the legal and judicial system, its failure to distinguish between more and less serious crimes or between wilful, flagrant violations by an officer and "good-faith" errors committed in difficult circumstances, its exclusion of the most credible kinds of evidence, its intensification of plea bargaining and its tendency to push the judiciary toward dangerously expanded notions of probable cause. We must now turn to alternatives to the rule to investigate what they offer us.

Notes

1. Oaks, *Studying the Exclusionary Rule in Search and Seizure,* 37 U. Chi. L. Rev. 665, 668 (1970).
2. 381 U.S. 618 (1965).
3. 414 U.S. 338 (1974).
4. Oaks, footnote 1, *supra,* 736-39, and Wingo, *Growing Disillusionment with the Exclusionary Rule,* 25 Sw. L.J. 573, 576 (1971), note the improper protection of the guilty afforded by the operation of the rule.

5. Oaks, footnote 1, *supra,* 736-39, notes that the rule provides no compensation to the innocent victims of illegal searches and seizures.

6. On this side of the balance must be weighed the debilitating fear in which members of society live if they believe that crime—both punished and unpunished—is so great as to pose a substantial danger. Such a fear is part of what makes crime a public problem, not a private one.

7. For a similar argument, see Barrett, *Exclusion of Evidence Obtained by Illegal Searches—A Comment on People v. Cahan,* 43 Calif. L. Rev. 565, 580-81 (1955). For a contrary argument, see Schrock and Welsh, *Up From Calandra: The Exclusionary Rule as a Constitutional Requirement,* 59 Minn. L. Rev. 251, 277-80 (1974). They argue: "If one can so readily lose his right to be free from promiscuous police invasions because of what those invasions reveal he has done in private, what besides arbitrary prejudice is to prevent the principle of waiver from having an effect also, for example, upon his right to silence or his right not to be placed twice in jeopardy, or, for that matter, his right to due process of law?" *Ibid.,* 278-79. Schrock and Welsh may be right as to the Fifth Amendment self-incrimination clause because it, like the search and seizure clause, addresses the means by which evidence may be taken from individuals. However, their argument is misguided as to the guarantees concerning double jeopardy, due process and, one could add to their list, fair trial. As has been argued, it is possible through the commission of crimes to forfeit the right to keep certain evidence in the private sphere; however, it is difficult to imagine what action by an individual would justify forfeiture of his rights concerning double jeopardy, due process, or a fair trial. One additional point as to self-incrimination and the right to silence must be made: exclusion of evidence in violation of the Fifth Amendment self-incrimination clause is often necessary in order to guard against convictions obtained on the basis of involuntary—and thus unreliable—statements or confessions. Thus, in many cases there are good reasons having nothing to do with considerations of privacy for excluding certain incriminating statements or confessions. See Schlesinger, *Witness Against Himself: The Fifth Amendment Self-Incrimination Clause as Public Policy,* 3 Claremont J. 55 (1975).

8. 116 U.S. 616 (1886).

9. *The Search and Seizure Probelm—Two Approaches: The Canadian Tort Remedy and the U.S. Exclusionary Rule,* 1 J. Police Sci. and Ad. 36, 37 (1973); the statistical evidence for the conclusion reported in the aforementioned article may be found in Spiotto, *Search and Seizure: An Empirical Study of the Exclusionary Rule and Its Alternatives,* 2 J. Legal Studies 243 (1973).

    Spiotto's research methodology is criticized in *Critique: On the Limitations of Empirical Evaluations of the Exclusionary Rule: A*

Critique of the Spiotto Research and U.S. v. Calandra, 69 Nw. U.L. Rev. 740, 740-76 (1974). But that critique, while it does point out certain weaknesses in Spiotto's work, underlines the basic difficulty with the rule: that "substantial police illegality continues even after adoption of the rule" 755, and that the rule is a weak deterrent. The critique argues correctly that Spiotto's research does not answer the question of how much more police illegality there would be without the rule.

Other empirical studies of the impact of the rule are: Katz, *The Supreme Court and the State: An Inquiry into Mapp v. Ohio in North Carolina,* 45 N.C.L. Rev. 119 (1966); Nagel, *Testing the Effects of Excluding Illegally Obtained Evidence,* 1965 Wisc. L. Rev. 283; and Weinstein, *Local Responsibility for Improvement of Search and Seizure Practices,* 34 Rocky Mt. L. Rev. 150 (1962). The findings of these studies are inconclusive because of the limited area from which data was gathered or because of indirect measures of behavior by law enforcement officials. Canon, *Is the Exclusionary Rule in Failing Health? Some New Data and a Plea Against A Precipitous Conclusion,* 62 Ky. L.J. 681, 686 (footnote 27) (1973-74). Thus, they are not discussed at length here.

Oaks, footnote 1, *supra,* 678-709, argues from empirical data that the rule has been a highly ineffective deterrent against illegal searches and seizures.

10. This table appears in Spiotto, *Search and Seizure,* footnote 9, *supra,* 247.
11. *Ibid.,* at 246 and 248.
12. Spiotto, *Search and Seizure Problem,* footnote 9, *supra,* 49.
13. Footnote 1, *supra.*
14. *Ibid.,* 685.
15. *Ibid.,* 689-93 and 707.
16. The figures appear in *Ibid.,* 690.
17. *Ibid.,* 755.
18. *The Impact of Mapp v. Ohio on Police Behavior* (delivered at the annual meeting of the Midwest Political Science Association, Chicago, May, 1973), and *Local Courts v. The Supreme Court: The Impact of Mapp v. Ohio* (delivered at the annual meeting of the American Political Science Association, New Orleans, September, 1973).
19. Footnote 9, *supra.*
20. *Ibid.,* 698-99.
21. *Ibid.,* 698-99.
22. *Ibid.,* 699-700.
23. *Ibid.,* 699.

24. *Ibid.,* 701-02.
25. *Ibid.,* 702-25.
26. *Ibid.,* 725-26.
27. 91 (1967) in Oaks, footnote 1, *supra,* 720.
28. See Lafave, *Arrest: The Decision to Take a Suspect Into Custody,*
     chs. 21-4 (1965); Skolnik, *Justice Without Trial,* 220 (1967); Miller,
     Prosecution: The Decision to Charge a Suspect with a Crime, 246-50
     (1969).
29. Note, *Effect of Mapp v. Ohio on Police Search and Seizure Practice in
     Narcotics Cases,* 4 Colum. J. L. and Soc. Prob. 87, 99-101 (1968) in-
     dicates that the desire by the police to avoid the enforcement difficul-
     ties created by the *Mapp* decision has led to increased use of techniques
     of patrol which violate constitutional search and seizure requirements.
     These violations are not brought to light in court because such "pre-
     ventive patrol" techniques seldom culminate in the arrest and trial of
     persons. The purpose of such techniques "is not only to talk with in-
     dividuals who may be suspected of having recently committed crimes
     but, more broadly, to find and confiscate dangerous weapons and to
     create an atmosphere of police omnipresence which will dissuade per-
     sons from attempting to commit crimes because of the likelihood of
     their being detected and apprehended." *President's Commission on
     Law Enforcement and Administration of Justice,* Task Force Report:
     The Police 40 (1967) in Note, *Effect of Mapp v. Ohio,* 100.
30. Skolnik, footnote 28, *supra,* ch. 3.
31. The empirical data in *Effect of Mapp v. Ohio on Police Search and
     Seizure Practice in Narcotics Cases,* footnote 29, *supra,* 91-6, indicates
     that police allegations as to how evidence was obtained changed after
     the *Mapp* decision, although actual police practices did not change sub-
     stantially. The data indicate that police officers often fabricate
     testimony to avoid the effects of *Mapp*-based motions to suppress
     illegally seized evidence. Also, Oaks, footnote 1, *supra,* 739-42, notes
     that the rule creates an incentive for lying by the police, and through
     interviews with police officials documents the most common types of
     situations in which police fabrication occurs.
32. Dash, *Cracks in the Foundation of Criminal Justice,* 41 Ill. L. Rev.
     385, 391-2 (1951), in Oaks, footnote 1, *supra,* 750.
33. *Irvine v. California,* 347 U.S. 128, 136 (1954).
34. *Bivens v. Six Unknown Named Agents,* 403 U.S. 388, 413 (1971)
     (Burger, C.J., dissenting).
35. A recent study "failed to reveal a single law enforcement agency where
     individual sanctions are tied to an application of the exclusionary rule."
     Oaks, footnote 1, *supra,* 710. "The officer was assured of the

sympathy of his superiors so long as he acted in conformity with administrative norms of police organization . . . ." *Ibid.,* 727.

36. Inbau, *Restrictions in the Law of Interrogations and Confessions,* 52 Nw. U.L. Rev. 77, 78 (1958).

37. Oaks, footnote 1, *supra,* 727.

38. Wilson, *Varieties of Police Behavior,* 31-2 (1968), in Oaks, footnote 1, *supra,* 728.

39. Lafave and Remington, *Controlling the Police: The Judge's Role in Making and Reviewing Law Enforcement Decisions,* 63 Mich. L. Rev. 987, 1005 (1965), in Oaks, footnote 1, *supra,* 730; see also Oaks, 730-31.

40. Oaks, footnote 1, *supra,* 731, note 193.

41. Burns, *Mapp v. Ohio: An All-American Mistake,* 19 DePaul L. Rev. 80, 95-6 (1969), in Oaks, footnote 1, *supra,* 723.

42. Oaks, footnote 1, *supra,* 688-89.

43. Oaks, footnote 1, *supra,* 726; Wingo, footnote 4, *supra,* 576, note, as argued above, that the real brunt of the rule falls on the prosecutor, not the police.

44. 367 U.S. 643, 655 (1961).

45. 338 U.S. 25, 44 (1949) (Murphy, J., dissenting) (the position of the dissent became the majority position in *Mapp*).

46. *Burdeau v. McDowell,* 256 U.S. 465, 477 (Brandeis, J., dissenting). See also *United States v. Calandra,* 414 U.S. 338, 357 (1974) (Brennan, J., dissenting).

47. *Silverthorne Lumber Co. v. United States,* 251 U.S. 385, 392 (1920). See also *United States v. Calandra,* footnote 46, *supra,* 357 (Brennan, J., dissenting).

48. *Ibid.,* 746.

49. *Restrictions in the Law of Search and Seizure,* 52 Nw. U.L. Rev. 46, 55 (1958).

50. See *Stone v. Powell,* 44 L.W. 5313, 5320 (1976).

51. Footnote 44, *supra.*

52. As to applying the exclusionary rule only in the most serious cases, see Kaplan, *The Limits of the Exclusionary Rule,* 26 Stan. L. Rev. 1027, 1046-49 (1974).

53. Both Wingo, footnote 4, *supra,* 577-78, and *Student Comment: The Tort Alternative to the Exclusionary Rule in Search and Seizure,* 63 Journal of Crim. L., C. and P.S. 256, 258-59 (1972), note that the rule fails in any way to take into account the seriousness of the violations committed by the police officer—whether the violation is a flagrant abuse or an understandable error of honest judgment, or

whether it results in a serious deprivation of the defendant's rights or is simply a harmless error.

54.   Footnote 44, *supra.*

55.   388 U.S. 263 (1957).

56.   Footnote 34, *supra,* 419. See Kamisar, *Wolf and Lustig, Ten Years Later: Illegal State Evidence in State and Federal Courts,* 43 Minn. L. Rev. 1083, 1146-47 (1959); and Wingo, footnote 4, *supra,* 577-78.

57.   Oaks, footnote 1, *supra,* 754-57; Satlin, *An Alternative to the Exclusionary Rule,* 26 JAG J. 255 (1971-72); and Spiotto, *Search and Seizure Problem,* footnote 9, *supra,* 39-49, urge strongly that, given the high costs and the ineffectiveness of the exclusionary rule, alternatives to the rule be seriously studied and implemented, at least for experimental purposes. Each author discusses specific types of alternatives to the rule.

58.   Alschuler, *The Prosecutor's Role in Plea Bargaining,* 36 U. Chi. L. Rev. 50, 56, 80-2 (1968), in Oaks, footnote 1, *supra,* 748.

59.   Barrett, *Personal Rights, Property Rights and the Fourth Amendment,* 1960 Sup. Ct. Rev. 46, 55; Kitch, *The Supreme Court's Possessive Code of Criminal Procedure,* 1969 Sup. Ct. Rev. 157-72, in Oaks, footnote 1, *supra,* 747.

It may be argued, as Justice Bradley did in *Boyd,* footnote 8, *supra,* that the Fifth Amendment prohibition on compulsory self-incrimination requires exclusion of illegally obtained evidence. Whatever the merits of this argument, the Fifth Amendment, like the Fourth, makes no provision for remedies or penalties in case of its violation; thus, the arguments made in this and the next chapter concerning methods of dealing with illegally obtained evidence are equally relevant to Fifth and Fourth Amendment violations.

It could be argued that the Supreme Court, in order to avoid the necessity of excluding probative evidence under the exclusionary rule, has dangerously expanded what the police may search or seize without a warrant. See *United States v. Watson,* 44 L.W. 4112 (1976) which involved a warrantless search in a situation in which the government conceded that there would have been time to secure a warrant; the Court held the search to be constitutional because it was based on probable cause and because the defendant, while in custody on a public street and after a warning that the fruits of the search could be used against him, had consented to it. See also *United States v. Santana,* 44 L.W. 4970 (1976) in which the Court held that a heroin suspect, initially observed by police officers as she stood in the doorway of her home, was subject to warrantless arrest and search inside her home. The Court reasoned that "hot pursuit" was necessary to prevent destruction of evidence and that the defendant could not defeat an otherwise proper arrest that had been set in motion in a public place by fleeing into a private one. Finally, see *South Dakota v. Opperman*, 44 L.W. 5294 (1976) in which the Court held constitutional a warrantless search of an automobile glove compartment conducted in the course of making an inventory of the objects of a car the police had impounded for parking violations.

objectives
① *deterrence*
② *method for compensating victims the innocent of illegal searches*
③ *conviction of guilty*

——— CHAPTER 4 ———

Alternatives to the Exclusionary Rule: A Proposal

Discussion of alternatives to the exclusionary rule must begin with the objectives to be achieved through their use. These are the deterrence of police misbehavior through identification and discipline of offending official(s), a better system than we have at present for compensating the innocent victims of illegal searches and seizures,[1] and conviction of the guilty—a result conspicuously lacking under the rule. These objectives require separate proceedings, a disciplinary proceeding against the offending police officer for deterrence and a civil-action proceeding for damages for compensation. Before discussing these in detail below, a few preliminary points should be made. The guilty victim has no claim to compensation for deprivation of privacy since his privacy, as argued before, has not been invaded. However, while the guilty victim would not be allowed to claim this kind of compensation for the invasion of Fourth Amendment rights, he would still have a civil cause of action if the police do unnecessary violence to his person or damage to his property; for although by his criminal activity he loses his right to privacy, he clearly retains other rights of person and property. Of course, we must discipline the offending officer, be the suspect guilty or innocent, because the officer has no way of knowing before he commits the illegal search and seizure whether the suspect is guilty or innocent, and because he has violated the rules of search and seizure.

What follows is my proposal for an alternative to the exclusionary rule which, I argue, would accomplish the proper objectives of the rule better than does the rule itself. Later in the chapter, two due-process arguments for the exclusionary rule will be discussed and, finally, some specific proposals will be advanced as to how we may move away from the rule as a remedy against police misbehavior.

The Independent Review Board

As to discipline of the offending officer, it is clear that prosecutors cannot be relied upon to institute proceedings against offending officers, because they rely heavily on a good relationship with the police in order to carry out their duties.[2] Thus, disciplinary action must be initiated and meted out from some other source. One possible source of such discipline would be the judiciary, aided by an independent review board.[3]

A hearing would be held (separately from the criminal trial of the victim of the search and seizure) before an independent review board which would investigate the nature and severity of the officer's misconduct. It would assess an appropriate punishment ranging from a fine to permanent severance from the police force. The board would take into account the record of the offending official, perhaps being more lenient to first offenders. Furthermore, evidence that the officer acted in good faith (without knowledge of wrongdoing) or evidence that he used reasonable force should be considered. At the review board hearing, there would need to be due-process protections for the suspect official, including representation by counsel; a special "prosecutor," entirely separate from the police or prosecutor's office, would have to be appointed in order to prevent any conflict-of-interest problems from arising with the "regular" prosecutor. This hearing would be disciplinary in nature, not criminal, but an officer might, in some instances, face additional criminal liability.

If a trial judge believed that there were evidence of illegal official behavior (regardless of the outcome of the trial), he could order such a hearing to be held. Under such a system, the judge must be particularly alert during testimony to the possibility of illegal behavior by officials, since defense counsel would not have the incentive of a suppression motion to bring forward illegal behavior. The judge must be given discretion to ask questions concerning how evidence was obtained in order to make sure that he has enough information to recommend, where necessary, a hearing on police misconduct. In addition to referral of possible misconduct by the judiciary, a citizen who is an innocent victim of illegal search and seizure, but who is never brought to trial involving this search, may report his complaint directly to the review board for investigation. Some jurisdictions might even wish to allow suspects, whether convicted or acquitted, to bring their own complaints directly to the board, though (because of anger at the police) this could lead to the filing of substantial numbers of less than meritorious complaints. Such a separate disciplinary hearing would provide an independent forum for investigation of police misconduct, unlike the present system in which police conduct is scrutinized by the judge as one of the numerous issues raised at trial. Such a proceeding, unlike the situation of a judge at trial, can give the misconduct question undivided attention and may well afford more time than a trial to resolve allegations of police misconduct.

Legislative bodies may wish to consider awarding a minimal, but automatic, compensation to the successful complainant as an incentive to bring the complaint; in doing this, however, the problem of encouraging less than meritorious complaints must be considered. Or, as an alternative method of encouraging victims to file complaints, a legislature may wish to allow admission to some degree of the results of the disciplinary hearing in a civil proceeding, though the problem here is that admission of such evidence may be prejudicial.

The functions set out above could be well accomplished by an independent review board made up of citizens, judges, law officers and any other groups whose representation may be desirable. The success of the plan depends on careful composition of the board with a view toward representing differing interests; methods of choosing members of the board could vary from place to place. Board members not on the police force will help to provide public and independent scrutiny of police work and will avoid the pitfalls of governmental self-scrutiny, so well illustrated in the recent Watergate and CIA revelations. In short, the "public members" will help to insure a certain responsiveness on the part of the police to the wishes of the community.

A board would be preferable to an exclusion hearing before a judge for two important reasons. First, as noted above, a board would have more time and resources available for investigating the facts of an alleged misbehavior than would normally be available to a judge while a trial is in progress. Second, a board would have the capacity to investigate the possibility that any of the offending officer's superiors had encouraged or ordered him to act as he did, and to take appropriate punitive action where such a pattern is found.

This proposed system would have the advantage of being paid for by the state and it would not need to depend upon the prosecutor or the possibly indigent victim of alleged misbehavior to initiate or sustain proceedings, but would, in most instances, be initiated by the judiciary. In some cases, the punishments meted out by the board might not be sufficiently severe, but it must be remembered that, under the exclusionary rule, it is extremely rare that direct sanctions are imposed on offending officers at all.

There is, of course, a problem with this procedure that cannot be entirely overcome: even if the courts and review boards were to supply counsel to all indigents who appeared before them, there would still remain the

problem of the credibility of evidence taken from a recently convicted felon.
Yet, if we are going to attempt to establish the degree of culpability of the
officer involved, this problem cannot be entirely circumvented. One partial
remedy would be for the review board or judge to require independent
evidence corroborating the convict's version. Also, though a convict may be
motivated by revenge, lying would not materially benefit him. This fact
would diminish his reasons for lying at this stage. In addition, one should
note that while it is true that in the absence of the rule, convicts may lie
about the circumstances of searches and seizures, it is equally true that
under the rule the suspect and convict may well wish to lie about those
circumstances, in order to have evidence suppressed at the trial or on appeal.
Since either presence or absence of the exclusionary rule may encourage
lying about the circumstances of searches and seizures, it would seem difficult, solely on the basis of truthfulness, to choose one over the other.

The above plan stresses the need for an independent or external review
of police conduct as opposed to internal self-review by the police. Although
internal imposition of discipline is quickest, most efficient (because investigation can be done on an in-house basis) and most likely to be accepted
(because it emanates from respected colleagues and friends),[4] there are a
number of compelling arguments against any system which relies on it
completely. First, the evidence suggests that with internal review meaningful discipline is rarely imposed on officers who are found to have committed
serious offenses.[5] For example, "Prior to the establishment of a citizen
Police Advisory Board, no Philadelphia officer had ever been disciplined on
the basis of a citizen complaint of police abuse."[6] Also, "Of thirty
brutality complaints to the Inspection Officer of the Newark Police Department in 1966-67, none resulted in a policeman's being charged."[7] Second,
minority and other disadvantaged groups who are most frequently the
victims of police abuse[8] are sometimes reluctant to file a complaint with
the very agency they believe has mistreated them. Finally, there are a
number of human, organizational, and bureaucratic factors which strongly
militate against serious internal review by police:

> The concept of internal review is also limited by the degree to
> which a departmental superior can suppress his natural feeling of
> loyalty toward his subordinates. Because he faces the possibility
> that concession to citizen demands will undermine the morale of
> his organization, even the conscientious police commissioner may
> encounter difficulty in properly handling complaints. Like most
> other entities, police departments have a self-interest to protect,
> and if a police department tacitly overlooks misconduct by its
> patrolmen, it cannot be expected to condemn itself publicly

through internal review mechanisms. In such a case, only an external organization can offer consistently impartial and objective review of allegations of police misconduct.[9]

Because of the difficulties of internal review, a number of cities have attempted citizen review boards—Philadelphia, New York City, Washington, and Rochester.[10] Because the Philadelphia Police Advisory Board (PAB) operated longer than the others, it presents the best case for analysis. PAB was able to achieve a number of important successes:

> It evidently achieved some degree of support from the minority communities where police presence was most irritating; one-half of all complaints were filed by Negroes in a city that is three-quarters white. Dispositions most frequently emerged from informal settlements. This conciliation process presumably permitted solutions acceptable to both citizen and officer with a minimum of the tensions normally incident to an adversary hearing. Furthermore, the complainant often sought only an apology or eradication of an unjustified arrest record.

> The PAB also submitted an annual report to the mayor which afforded it an opportunity to influence broad police policies and identify the most persistent sources of citizen irritation. As a result of this report, definitive guidelines for proper use of handcuffs were established, and steps were taken to rectify apparent patterns of mistreatment of apprehended persons at station houses and discourtesy directed at citizens making inquiries.[11]

There were, however, some substantial difficulties, many of which are addressed by the disciplinary plan proposed here. Complaints were comparatively few and sporadic.[12] The provision in our proposal for automatic referral by the trial judge would be helpful in this area. PAB sometimes found itself constructing a case for a complainant without counsel, and this procedure did little to impart an image of fairness.[13] The provision in our plan for all complainants and suspect officers to have counsel, provided by the government, if necessary, should alleviate the difficulty. Further, the Philadelphia experience strongly indicates the advisability of the board having some investigative staff independent of the police; in Philadelphia, police investigations resulted in delays and a backlog of unresolved cases, none of which contributed to the positive image of the board.[14] Also, the experience of PAB demonstrates the need for careful construction of strong and unambiguous enabling legislation, since the work of PAB was suspended in part due to a weak charter.[15]

Police antagonism toward such review boards is well known, and
Philadelphia was no exception:

> Probably the real reason for this hostility is that policemen
> fiercely resent being singled out among all other local govern-
> ment officials for civilian review. Implicit in such a board's
> very existence seems to be an assumption that policemen are
> characteristically arbitrary or brutal and have to be watched.
> Since policemen apparently believe that civilian review boards
> symbolize society's contemptuous discrimination against them,
> the ill feeling the institution provokes may not be worth the
> benefits it confers.[16]

This hostility toward external review cannot, of course, be eliminated but
can perhaps be lessened. As suggested before, police officers and officials
should be represented on the board so that the policeman's perspective is
necessarily taken into account. Also, a number of arguments can be made
to the police in support of such a board: first, the existence and fair,
efficient operation of the board does much to improve the image of the
police in the community; second, it can be argued that police, as noted
above, are singled out for civilian review because of the great importance
of their work and its impact on all citizens—this point should gratify the
officer by reminding him of the central role he plays in community life.
Third, if the review board operates successfully, it should support the police
contention that "bad apples" are few and far between in their ranks. And
finally, if investigations by the board are perceived by the police as being
impartial and fair, they may be more satisfied than they are with the
current exclusion policy, and this satisfaction may have salutary effects on
the maintenance of discipline and the avoidance of misbehavior within the
police force.

Finally, in Philadelphia, the adversary nature of the proceedings before
PAB sometimes served to exacerbate police-community relations.[17] Two
points must be made about this: first, anything less than a full adversary
proceeding can lead to charges of unfairness on the part of the board, as
happened in Philadelphia; second, if our purpose is to give a full airing to
complaints against the police and to the police response to these complaints,
there seems no real alternative to the adversary process.

The above proposal will not lead to the imposition of discipline on all
misbehaving officers. But since suppression of evidence has led to the discipline of almost no one, the proposal made here seems to be a real improvement over the exclusionary rule.

The Civil Remedy

In addition to police discipline, the innocent victim should have a means by
which to collect compensation for an illegal search and seizure, and to point
out official misbehavior. The potential for substantial "penalty compensation"[18]—an amount large enough to make the filing of the suit and its
attendant responsibilities worthwhile—would go far to correct the problem
of insufficient incentive for counsel to point out official misbehavior.

Specifically, I suggest a statutory civil action with provision for the
award of monetary compensation, the amount depending on the gravity of
the misbehavior (but with a minimum amount to be awarded in the event
that any violation is found). Such an action would allow innocent victims
to recover a basic compensatory amount plus counsel's fees without any
showing of specific damage to the victim or flagrant violation by the
officer. The only proof necessary would be a showing that the victim's
Fourth Amendment rights had been violated; the greater the invasion of
Fourth Amendment rights, the higher the compensation. The seriousness
of the invasion, and thus the amount of compensation, would be measured
by the amount of mental or physical suffering and inconvenience caused a
victim of improper procedure, as well as the degree to which an officer
violated clear rules governing proper searches and seizures. There are now
in existence state common law causes of action under which victims may
recover damages, but civil actions are rarely instituted (and even more rarely
won) because it is necessary to show either substantial harm to the victim (for
compensatory damages) or outrageous official misconduct (for punitive
damages).[19] Winning the proposed civil suit would be easier because no such
showing would be necessary. This plan would provide an economic incentive
for victims and for lawyers to bring to public attention cases of official misconduct, as well as provide an avenue for compensation. Victims of illegal
searches and seizures would be encouraged to bring suit because the regularized
procedure suggested here, designed precisely for such victims, would help to
overcome reluctance to sue the police. Under existing institutional arrangements,
free legal counsel could be provided for indigent persons who wish to bring
this type of action.[20]

From where should the money come to pay the victim if he wins the
proposed statutory civil action? I believe it must come from the public
treasury of whatever unit of government is involved.[21] If the amounts
awarded were considerable enough, superior officers would be discouraged
from "making it worthwhile" (through increased pay or promotion) for sub-
ordinates to effect illegal searches and seizures. If the public were required
to pay for such police escapades in the form of substantial damages taken

from general tax revenues, the public would take a dim view of such police activity[22]; predictably, corrective pressure would be brought to bear on the police. Also, law enforcement officers would hardly be overjoyed were public money to be awarded to criminal suspects.[23] It is worth considering whether the plaintiff should be permitted to collect damages directly from the errant officer, since the threat of such damages would serve, at least in some instances, as a deterrent against offical misbehavior. However, individual liability of the officer must not be so imposing that it prevents him from acting where action is necessary. In any event, the errant officer would be subject to discipline imposed by the independent review board.

Both civil litigation involving police misconduct and the proposed disciplinary hearing give rise to a common problem. A police officer can use his various discretionary powers—the power of arrest, the threat to file a criminal complaint, the power to harrass—in order to cover up his own illegal activity. That is, an officer may attempt to prevent an innocent victim of his misconduct, from bringing a complaint through the means noted above.[24] The exoneration from possible criminal charges may provide sufficient personal relief to the defendant that he may not be motivated to pursue further legal action against the police officer. The response to this difficulty is that whenever one attempts to hold the police responsible for their misconduct, certain officers will attempt to evade that responsibility; this is not a reason for refusing to hold police responsible. The fact that individuals attempt to evade application to themselves of legitimate rules is not *per se* a reason for abandoning those rules.

The proposed civil remedy presents several problems. First, states and localities would have to forego the protection of sovereign immunity, i.e., voluntarily assume liability for police torts related to the Fourth Amendment.[25] As argued before, public liability for such torts might well bring significant pressure on the police to refrain from misconduct. In addition, public liability is crucial; individual officers may not have the resources to pay substantial judgments, or juries may often perceive this to be the case—whether it is or not. Indeed, there is evidence that officers are often judgment-proof to the extent that they are unable to pay substantial damages.[26] Government liability would be one way to assure potential defendants of sufficient funds to pay damages. In addition, in response to effective civil remedies against police misbehavior, police may desire, and be able, to purchase liability insurance covering their conduct as police officers; such insurance is currently available in many jurisdictions from a number of commercial carriers. While such insurance would mitigate the financial impact of successful civil actions on police, it would also expose the police officer to rate increases and policy cancellation, if he lost a civil case as a result of misbehavior.

Both the federal government and the states have moved in the direction of assuming liability for the misconduct of their officials. Kenneth Culp Davis points out, "During the last fifteen years, courts of twelve states and the District of Columbia have imposed tort liability by judicial action on either state or local governments for some types of deliberate torts, and thirteen states have done so by legislation."[27] Indeed, *Bivens*[28] held that petitioners are entitled to collect money damages from the federal government as a result of invasion of privacy by federal officials.

It is sometimes alleged that government liability for police misconduct would have little deterrent effect on misconduct since the individual officer would feel no ill effects. Two points must be made: first, the general proposal made here does not rely exclusively on civil litigation for its deterrent effect, but rather on both civil litigation and the review board. Second, though some critics of the rule doubt the deterrent effect of government liability for police torts,[29] there is some evidence of a deterrent effect "found in the industrial safety field . . . where imposition of liability has the effect of forcing the employer to isolate accident-prone employees from situations where an accident might result."[30]

The tort remedy with government liability for damages may face substantial political opposition in the form of the unwillingness of taxpayers to assume the burden[31] and that opposition will be especially strong when it is perceived that damages are paid to disreputable persons or even formerly convicted felons. The response to this is that our Bill of Rights makes certain guarantees upon which citizens have a right to rely; when these guarantees are violated through police misconduct, the *innocent* victims must be compensated by the public treasury because it was the public's agents who committed the violation. The argument must be made to unhappy taxpayers that, where possible, constitutional violations committed by the state's agents must be remedied. Further, those who complain can be reminded that the alternative to the plan proposed here is the release of countless guilty persons and thus more "crime in the streets."

It is said that tort actions for police misconduct have traditionally been hard to win, because the officer can assert the defenses of good faith and reasonable force.[32] But since, under the civil action proposed here, the ability of the complainant to win damages depends solely on whether his Fourth Amendment rights have been violated, good faith will not be a defense as to guilt or innocence—either a violation took place or it did not.

Although reasonable force may be a factor in computing damages, it is clearly not a complete defense against an illegal search. While such factors as good faith, excessive force, the reputation of the plaintiff, or his previous criminal record should not be considered in determining the verdict, they may have some relevance to the amount of damages awarded. Indeed, in common law actions for trespass, mitigation of damages are permitted where poor reputation can be demonstrated.

Another problem with the civil remedy may be the predictable unwillingness of lawyers to litigate because of the low probability of success.[33] This low probability results from the high standards of proof required in most current actions—substantial harm and/or outrageous official conduct. But since in the action proposed, the standard of proof required for a judgment favoring the plaintiff is simply the existence of a Fourth Amendment violation, this difficulty is reduced. It is also said that some lawyers will not wish to damage their relations with police by litigating such actions. This is obviously a serious problem, though perhaps in view of current trends, it will become less serious as time passes. Legal education today increasingly stresses the obligations of the legal profession to society and there has been a general movement of law school graduates into public interest and *pro bono* litigation.[34] If this trend continues, the number of lawyers ready and able to bring police misconduct litigation will be adequate, although the supply of such attorneys will obviously be greater in large cities than in small towns.

An additional problem is that minority groups and the poor, who seem to be most affected by police misconduct, would have, on the one hand, the greatest need for the civil remedy and, on the other, the greatest difficulty in attempting to use it—lack of money, distrust of the police and the legal system, and fear of retaliation.[35] In response to these difficulties, one can only make a maximum effort to provide free legal counsel and general information concerning this kind of civil action in the community. Under our system, disadvantaged persons cannot be forced to litigate against their will; but they can be provided with the means to litigate, if they so desire, through free legal services and court-appointed attorneys. While it is true that the poor suffer disproportionately from deprivation of legal services, such deprivation is a general problem which needs public attention—it is not in itself an argument against the creation of a new and more effective remedy against police misconduct.

Not every aggrieved individual is willing to institute a law suit. The civil plaintiff must bear attorney costs which may be prohibitive for the typical victim of police misconduct. Also, a potential plaintiff may be skeptical about the availability of legal relief and fearful of retaliatory prosecution and retribution by the police. Also, the notoriously slow operation of civil machinery may eliminate the impatient citizen who seeks rapid redress of his grievances.[36] These difficulties would to some extent be mitigated by the increasing availability of *pro bono* lawyers, some of whom would be disposed to take on police misconduct litigation, by the increasing trend toward legal help for the middle class,[37] by the willingness of some attorneys to make their fees contingent on an award, and by the recent acceleration of the civil calenders in some jurisdictions.

Even if the evidence presents an objectively strong case, a judge or jury may be willing to tolerate some acts of police misconduct. "If the plaintiff is poor, uneducated, or has a criminal record, his credibility will be low."[38] A jury may conclude that his "type" does not deserve a judgment against an officer of the law. Even if the plaintiff wins his case, beyond compensation for physical injuries, he may have little to gain. The victim "may not have substantial earnings or reputation to lose"[39] for which he could be otherwise compensated. As Caleb Foote suggests, for most potential tort claimants, "the moral aspects of the case" tend to reduce recoveries. Claimants against the police apparently lack the "minimum elements of respectability" upon which humiliation, pain, suffering, and loss of reputation can be based.[40] Thus "a plaintiff's prior reputation, economic status, and even his demeanor in court can suggest that he is undeserving of substantial reparation."[41] On the other hand, it should be added that a plaintiff's reputation, economic status and courtroom behavior will influence the outcome or award in virtually all kinds of civil cases; police misconduct litigation is not an exception.

Despite these problems, there are a number of factors which suggest that a civil remedy is viable. In recent years, there has been a sizeable increase in the number of federal police misconduct cases brough under section 1983 of the Civil Rights Act of 1871. "This statute makes any person who, under color of state law, causes a citizen to be deprived of the rights, privileges or immunities guaranteed by federal law liable to the injured party."[42] Section 1983 reads,

> Every person who, under color of any statute, ordinance, regulation, custom, or usage, of any State or Territory, subjects, or causes to be subjected, any citizen of the United States or other person within the jurisdiction thereof to the deprivation of any rights, privileges, or immunities secured by the Constitution and laws, shall be liable to the party injured in an action at law, suit in equity, or other proper proceeding for redress.[43]

Thus, recovery may be had against a police officer under this statute, even when the plaintiff has not been subjected to physical violence. The police officer is liable if there was a deprivation of a constitutional right, privilege, or immunity under "color of law." The celebrated 1961 case of *Monroe v. Pape*[44] held an illegal search and seizure by the Chicago police to be actionable under Section 1983. The Supreme Court in *Monroe* applied a liberal construction to "color of law,":

> Misuse of power, possessed by virtue of state law and made possible only because the wrongdoer is clothed with the authority of state law, is action taken 'under color of' state law.[45]

> This standard includes the acts of a police officer who can show no authority whatever for his action. And even action contrary to state law is under color of law if the policeman is clothed with the indices of state authority.[46]

Federal courts disagree as to whether, under 1983 actions, good faith, or nonwillfulness, or reasonable force should constitute a defense.[47]

Monroe v. Pape is also typical of the kind of case for which recovery may be sought under Section 1983.

> In this case, 13 Chicago police officers broke into the home of a Negro family in the early morning, routed them from bed, made them stand naked in the living room, and ransacked every room, emptying drawers and ripping mattress covers. Mr. Monroe was then taken to the police station and detained on 'open' charges for ten hours, while he was interrogated. He was not taken before a magistrate, though one was accessible; he was not permitted to call his family or an attorney. He was subsequently released without criminal charges being preferred against him. The officers had no search warrant and no arrest warrant. They acted 'under color' of the statutes and ordinances of Illinois and the city of Chicago. On these uncontroverted facts, Mr. & Mrs. Monroe ultimately collected $11,000 in damages after litigation in the federal courts.[48]

Several important holdings were issued in *Monroe* which are important for subsequent cases under section 1983. They are:

1. Defendants need not have had a specific intent to violate plaintiff's civil rights; Section 1983 "should be read against the background of tort liability that makes a man responsible for the natural consequences of his actions."[49]

2. The existence of a state remedy does not preclude the federal action. Hence, state and federal law provide alternative routes to recovery for the same wrongful conduct.[50]

3. Municipalities are not "persons" within the meaning of Section 1983 and therefore cannot be sued under it.[51]

The collection of damages by the Monroes reflects the utility of seeking monetary compensation in some cases of police misconduct. However, some postjudgment factors come to light which ironically emphasize the lack of a deterrent effect of civil tort actions, whether brought under state law or under Section 1983, and which emphasize the need for the kind of separate disciplinary proceedings recommended here. While the Supreme Court held Officer Pape liable for a deliberate tort, "the City of Chicago paid the judgment, did not even reprimand Pape, and retired him with honors in 1973."[52]

Moreover, Ginger and Bell report that similar actions under Section 1983 seeking monetary compensation against the misconduct of police officers have been successful in at least 54 cases between 1950 and 1967; some of these cases fall in the area of search and seizure.[53] For example, in *McArthur v. Pennington,*[54] $5,100 in damages were awarded to the plaintiffs on various complaints, including an illegal search of their trunks. In *Lucero v. Donovan,*[55] a Mexican-American woman won $5,000 after a nonjury trial on her complaint of an illegal search and seizure.[56] This approach will not compensate all victims of all illegal searches and seizures, only some of those who file claims. But what has been said here indicates that individuals can collect damages in police misconduct litigation. The civil action proposed here attempts, where possible, to eliminate some of the legal difficulties faced by earlier plaintiffs and thus render the civil remedy available, practical, and fair.

Further, as noted in Chapter 2, the Supreme Court has held in *Bivens*[57] that, even in the absence of Section 1983, the Fourth Amendment itself creates a federal cause of action and the possibility of damages. This creates another avenue for police misconduct litigation in regard to search and seizure violation.

Finally, Section 1983 has afforded an additional remedy and deterrent against police misconduct in a few cases, namely, a judicial injunction against specified conduct by police officials.[58] Since these injunctions have been handed down rarely and since there seem to be numerous and severe problems with them,[59] they will not be discussed here. Civil remedies and a review board of the kind proposed here seems to provide a more promising means for dealing with police misconduct, though in some cases injunctions may be appropriate.

To sum up, despite the problems of civil actions discussed above, Section 1983 actions offer substantial demonstration that the civil route is not at all blocked. These actions show that individuals can, and have, collected substantial amounts of money in police misconduct litigation and that if, as is attempted in the proposal made here, unfair obstacles to success in such suits are removed, the civil remedy offers real promise as a component of a meaningful system of disciplining our police.

Arguments for the Proposal As a Whole

A few general words are in order in support of this approach as a whole, combining as it does discipline of the police with compensation of innocent victims. It should be noted that not all criminal court judges who are faced with evidence that should be excluded, in fact, exclude it. It is well known among lawyers that evidence must reek badly before some judges will exclude it and judges vary widely in their views as to what is or is not a reasonable search and seizure. Thus, we must pose some additional questions about the actual operation of the rule, and we must have a greater willingness to try other approaches.

It may be argued that the above plan will multiply the number of hearings and procedures in the criminal process and will consequently increase the expense of the administration of justice. This is undoubtedly true: the reply to it is simply that in criminal justice, as in most other things, we get what we pay for.

A very important advantage of the proposal for review boards and civil remedies is that it is readily applicable to grand jury proceedings; the Supreme Court held in *Calandra* that the exclusionary rule does not apply to questions based on illegally obtained evidence at the grand jury level, thus severely limiting the scope of the rule at that level. Under the proposed system, the judge presiding over the grand jury proceedings could refer errant officers to the review board, just as he could at trial; indeed, some legislatures might wish to allow both those indicted and those freed by the grand jury to bring their complaints to the review board, though less-than-meritorious complaints caused by anger at the police are a real possibility in such situations. In addition, unindicted suspects could well file suits for damages as described here (though those indicted would have to await the outcome of their trial, since only innocent victims of illegal practices have the right to sue for deprivation of privacy, as argued above).

A question could well be raised as to how one would attempt to demonstrate that the proposal made here, if adopted, would be more effective than earlier methods. This presents a difficult problem: to some extent, a substantial number of proceedings before independent review boards and numerous civil actions—a reasonable proportion of them successful for the complainant—would be indicative of success. Yet, over a relatively long period of time, statistics of this kind could indicate that police misbehavior has not been reduced and that the plan is less than successful. Thus, the problem of evaluation for this, like other complex reforms, would not be easy to solve.

It is not possible to elaborate all the details of these proposals here, for many of these must be worked out in practice; nor is it possible to answer all possible objections to this kind of proposal. Nevertheless, the preceding proposals are submitted as a method by which we can move away from the difficulties and shortcomings of the exclusionary rule. As the legal literature makes clear, plans like the ones reviewed have been employed only rarely, and even then there was no real incentive to make them work, since most of the states, prior to *Mapp*,[60] had not experienced the great costs of the exclusionary rule—the alternative to the kind of plan proposed here. Ironically, there is the other side of the coin, namely, that the *Mapp* decision has largely removed from the states the incentive to deal with illegal search and seizure by means other than suppression. As Oaks points out: "By a peculiar form of federal preemption, the *Mapp* decision may sap state officials' energy and determination to control law enforcement officials in alternative ways that might prove just as effective and even more comprehensive than the exclusionary rule. Thus, The President's Crime Commission Task Force Report on the Police observed that the police administrator is ambivalent about the degree of his responsibility for controlling improper law enforcement behavior by his personnel . . . ."[61]

The present system of exclusion does not deter police misbehavior, nor does provide it compensation to the innocent: it simply frees many who are guilty and who, we have argued, have no legitimate claim to that freedom on the basis of invasion of privacy. The recommendations outlined above are intended to move us closer to a system which deters misconduct and compensates those who deserve compensation. There are obvious difficulties with the scheme proposed here which, like any system, will not deal properly with all violations, but at least a substantial number of officers could be disciplined and a substantial number of innocent victims of illegal procedures could be compensated. This is more than one can say for the present system of exclusion.

Two Due Process Arguments Concerning the Rule

The foregoing proposal has been presented as a pragmatic alternative which would better accomplish the objectives now purportedly served by the exclusionary rule. Two arguments relating to due process on behalf of the rule "in principle" require further discussion.

Proponents of the exclusionary rule claim that, through enforcement of the rule, our courts gain popular respect because they uniformly refuse to accept illegally obtained, "tainted" evidence; the theory seems to be that, were the courts to accept such evidence, they would be condoning the methods used to obtain it.[62] Through their refusal to admit illegally obtained evidence, the argument goes, the courts demonstrate their unswerving commitment to Fourth Amendment restrictions on search and seizure. This sense of commitment is communicated to police, causing them to refrain from illegal searches and seizures, and to citizens, causing them to respect the judicial system. A related argument, because it concerns the propriety of government activity, is that courts should not tolerate the government's benefiting from its own wrongdoing.

Two points must be made concerning these arguments. First, does a court not *lose* the respect of citizens when, through its enforcement of the exclusionary rule, it implicates itself in the freeing of a suspect in whose case reliable evidence has been obtained, albeit improperly, indicating that the suspect has committed a serious crime or crimes? Do the courts not *lose* respect when they implicate themselves in a situation so structured that law enforcement officers feel tremendous pressure to commit perjury?

Second, courts surely have a duty to support Fourth Amendment rights, due process, and fair play, but they also have a duty to pursue the truth—to free the innocent and convict the guilty. Under the exclusionary rule, the courts may claim to fulfill only the former duty. Under the system proposed above, the courts to a large extent fulfill both: they clearly express their commitment to Fourth Amendment search and seizure restrictions through their participation in the process of finding and punishing official misbehavior by law enforcement authorities, and they express their commitment to pursuing the truth by judging evidence solely on the basis of its reliability. One hopes it is not asking too much that our courts concern themselves not only with the privacy problems raised by the Fourth Amendment search and seizure clause but also with their general obligation to fairly establish guilt or innocence in criminal cases.

Also, in a real sense, courts would tolerate government wrongdoing (and the "benefits" that government derives from it) less under the proposed system than they do at present since they would participate directly, through the review board and civil damage suits, in a system which would deter wrongdoing more effectively than it is deterred now. At present, judges participate in a system in which no discipline or punishment is given to an officer whose misbehavior gives rise to exclusion; the judiciary has become part of a system in which misbehavior by law enforcement officials is rampant, apparently not decreasing significantly, and often tolerated or encouraged by superiors. Under the proposed system, the courts would become an integral part of a meaningful deterrent against official misbehavior. This is an improvement, and to the extent that the argument that government should derive no benefit from its wrongdoing is founded on the fear that such benefits would break down any deterrence mechanism (and therefore provide an incentive for wrongdoing), it should be remembered that a system without the rule, such as the one proposed here, would seem to provide a stronger deterrent than the present system of exclusion.

Under the proposed system, the government would obtain some convictions on the basis of improperly obtained evidence (though the stronger deterrent should substantially reduce official misbehavior). The courts would permit these convictions because of their commitment to conviction of the guilty and acquittal of the innocent, just as they would refer errant law enforcement officers to the disciplinary board because of their commitment to fair play, due process, and the deterrence of illegal practices. Such a procedure would strike a better balance between the various objectives of the judiciary than the present, one-sided concern with procedural and evidentiary problems.

The Path Away from the Rule

The exclusionary rule seems to be so deficient and the alternatives sufficiently promising that we should cease clinging to the rule. Indeed, the rule does not in any substantial way do what the alternatives would—directly punish offending officers and provide compensation to innocent victims of illegal law enforcement activity—and it has at least one serious liability not attached to the alternatives: it releases otherwise convictable and possibly dangerous persons on society.

The practical problem is, of course, how do we move away from the rule as a monolithic remedy for police misconduct? As was pointed out earlier, if the exclusionary rule were simply abandoned without substitute, the police might infer that all constitutional restraints had been removed and that, in effect, open season had been declared on criminal suspects. Chief Justice Burger suggests that Congress should formulate substitutes, as it did in 1946 with the Federal Tort Claims Act, which provides a form of relief for those with claims against the federal government.[63] If such substitutes were successful, the states might then wish to follow the federal model.

In addition, Chief Justice Burger made the specific proposal in his *Bivens* dissent that Fourth Amendment violations be made actionable in themselves and proposed that Congress codify this kind of remedy.[64] Although this proposal obviously moves in the right direction as to compensation, it leaves the question of discipline or punishment of the offending officer subject to uncertain and indirect pressures. Whether public liability for police misconduct would lead to proper discipline is, as noted before, a debatable matter; it is precisely for this reason that the plan proposed here provides for a separate disciplinary hearing. The Burger plan leaves the matter of direct discipline in uncertain form.

A number of alternatives to the present operation of the rule have been proposed in Congress for the federal jurisdiction, and their implementation would require revision of the rules announced in *Boyd*[65] and *Weeks*,[66] as would federal implementation of the proposal made here. In 1971, Senator Lloyd Bentsen of Texas proposed that evidence should not be excluded from any federal criminal proceeding solely because that evidence was obtained in violation of the Fourth Amendment, unless a court determines that, as a matter of law, such violations were substantial; this bill sets forth those circumstances that a court shall consider in making such a determination.[67] In 1972, former Congressman Lawrence Hogan of Maryland proposed a very similar bill in the House of Representatives.[68] Then in late 1972 and early 1973, Senator Bentsen and Congressman Gunn McKay of Utah proposed bills which, like the earlier ones described above, proposed to exclude the fruits of only substantial violations. But these bills contained at least one important feature not found in the earlier proposals: they provided that the United States be liable for illegal searches and seizures conducted either directly by agents of the federal government or indirectly, through others, at federal direction or request. The bills authorized punitive damages to be awarded in such actions and limited recovery to $25,000, including actual and punitive damages. Finally, the bills provided that the District Courts of the United States have exclusive jurisdiction over claims brought under these acts (the bills also placed a maximum on attorneys' fees in litigation undertaken pursuant to these acts).[69] Most recently, in September of 1973, and again in March 1975, Congressman Sam Steiger of Arizona proposed a bill similar to the Bentsen and McKay bills, with the exception that no dollar limit was placed on recovery by the victim of the illegal search and seizure.[70] None of these bills was enacted into law by Congress. Table 1 summarizes the legislative proposals introduced in Congress.

Table 1 Congressional Bills*

Date	Bill	Sponsor	Provisions
1971	S2657	Senator Bentsen, Texas	No evidence should be excluded from federal criminal proceedings unless it was obtained by means of a substantial violation of the Fourth Amendment; sets out circumstances for federal courts to consider in determining whether such a violation is substantial
1972	HR13682	Former Congressman Hogan, Maryland	Similar to S2657
1972	S881	Senator Bentsen, Texas	Similar to S2657, but also provided that the United States be liable for illegal searches and seizures conducted by its agents up to $25,000 and provided a maximum attorney's fee in cases brought pursuant to this statute; also gave U.S. District Courts exclusive jurisdiction over actions brought under this statute
1973	HR17096	Congressman Gunn McKay, Utah	Similar to S881
1973	HR10275	Congressman Sam Steiger, Utah	Similar to S881, but provided no dollar limit on recovery for illegal searches and seizures
1975	HR5628	Congressman Sam Steiger, Utah	Similar to HR10275

*None of these bills has been enacted into law by Congress.

These bills contain a number of positive features: first, they distinguish between substantial and insubstantial violations and thus invoke the rule only in those cases where the official violation is shown to be substantial, thus, these bills would not require that guilty persons be released in those cases where the rights of the accused had not been seriously violated. This feature of the bills responds to the defect in the present operation of the rule pointed out in the previous chapter, i.e., that it operates regardless of the seriousness of the violation. The Supreme Court in a recent case seemed to be moving in the direction of accepting the "substantial violation rule" for confessions;[71]

as Mr. Justice Rehnquist said, speaking for himself and seven other justices, "Just as the law does not require that a defendant receive a perfect trial, only a fair one, it cannot realistically require that policemen investigating serious crimes make no errors whatsoever. The pressure of law enforcement and the vagaries of human nature would make such an expectation unrealistic."[72] In the area of search and seizure, on June 25, 1975, the Supreme Court handed down a decision in *United States v. Peltier*.[73] In this case, the Court held that its previous decision in *Almeida-Sanchez v. United States*,[74] which ruled that a warrantless auto search about 25 miles from the Mexican border by Border Patrol agents without probable cause was unconstitutional, did not apply retroactively to such warrantless searches before June 1973, the date *Almeida-Sanchez* was handed down. Mr. Justice Rehnquist, writing for the majority, said that the major rationale underlying the rule—deterrence of improper law enforcement practices—does not require retroactive application where the agents were acting in good faith—that is, in reliance on a federal statute supported by longstanding administrative regulation. Mr. Justice Rehnquist said, "If the purpose of the exclusionary rule is to deter unlawful police conduct, then evidence obtained from a search should be suppressed only if it can be said that the law enforcement officer had knowledge, or may properly be charged with knowledge, that the search was unconstitutional . . . ."[75] At present, the exclusionary rule excludes all illegally obtained evidence, regardless of whether the officer acted in "good faith." Thus, Mr. Justice Rehnquist's view—apparently now the majority view on the court—would substantially restrict the application of the rule, if it were in the future to become law through a decided case. While this "good faith" distinction is not what this book recommends, it— like the substantial violation rule—shows an awareness, at the highest level, of the great difficulties and liabilities of the exclusionary rule.

A second laudable feature of these bills is that they make serious attempts to lay out the criteria which the federal judiciary should use in determining whether a violation is substantial; thus, judges will have some guidance in making these difficult determinations and will be less open to charges of caprice, arbitrariness, and inconsistency. And finally, some of these bills provide for compensation to the victims of illegal searches and seizures—and this sort of legislation is long overdue.

Yet, I believe, the bills contain a number of serious weaknesses—weaknesses which do not appear in the alternative to the rule described in this essay. First, the bills continue to contemplate use of the exclusionary rule in cases of substantial violation despite the high costs to society (e.g., releasing countless guilty persons), despite all the evidence noted in this essay that the rule is an ineffective deterrent, and despite all the other liabilities of the rule noted here. Second, the bills provide little or no deterrent for violations deemed by the courts to be insubstantial; this fact could encourage a careless attitude toward detail on the part of law enforcement officials, and might even encourage police to see what can be gotten away with before the courts draw the line on what is a substantial violation. Finally, the bills offer compensation to innocent *and* guilty victims of illegal searches and seizures; as argued above, persons whose guilt is established in whole or in part by illegally seized evidence should not be entitled to compensation, because their privacy has not been invaded. In general, although these bills in some respects move in the right direction, they also present a number of serious weaknesses which are not found in the alternative proposed here.

But just as important as these proposals from Congress, the arguments made here suggest that the Supreme Court should cease to insist upon exclusion of the fruits of improper state searches and seizures. There is nothing to stop the states from enacting alternative schemes along the lines suggested here and having them tested before the Supreme Court. Indeed, the Court might encourage submission of alternatives as part of a general movement away from *Mapp*.[76] It would be well for the Court to consolidate and take such cases as quickly as possible, first to establish new guidelines as to what kinds of alternatives will be accepted, and second so that states will not be encouraged to use unsatisfactory substitutes for the rule as part of a dilatory tactic designed to circumvent *Mapp*.[77] The Court should quickly dispose of those plans which seem to be patent attempts to avoid dealing with police misbehavior; on the other hand, it may wish to allow more time for adequate testing of *bona fide* plans which offer real promise of success. Court actions of this kind would have a number of substantial benefits; first, the diversity of experience among the states would give us and the courts some real evidence of how the exclusionary rule operates compared to its alternatives. Second, such developments might move us closer to an effective law enforcement system and further away from the irrational and capricious results of the operation of the exclusionary rule.

Allowing the states to try different kinds of approaches to the problem of official misconduct would, of course, not appeal to those who believe that the conduct of criminal justice should be everywhere uniform. But there are three considerations which those who favor such uniformity must bear in mind. First, as I have pointed out, the consequences of trying alternatives to the rule are not yet clear. We must try alternatives at the state level and then use the knowledge gained from the experiment to guide our future attempts to deter official misconduct. It has been suggested in this chapter that successful alternatives would involve a combination of discipline imposed on police by an independent review board with an improved civil remedy for those victims of illegal police practices who are not convicted in trials in which the seized evidence is admitted. Second, because crime is primarily the concern of the states, despite the growth in federal criminal law, it can be argued that the states should have more flexibility in law enforcement than the federal government.

Third, there is now considerable legal precedent for allowing local communities much latitude in dealing with their own problems. The school integration and busing opinions of the Supreme Court have consistently stressed that solutions must be designed to meet local conditions[78]; in a recent pornography decision, communities are allowed leeway in imposing "community standards" on books, films, etc., so long as material having clear social, political, or artistic value is not suppressed.[79] Finally, and perhaps most interesting, the Court of Appeals of the 5th Circuit in *Hawkins v. Town of Shaw,*[80] having found that Shaw, Mississippi, engaged in systematic and *de jure* discrimination in the distribution of town services against its black population, ordered that the town propose its own remedies to rectify that discrimination and report these back to the Court within a specified period of time. In case no plan was submitted or no progress were made pursuant to the plan in the specified period, then the Court reserved the right to impose its own plan to end discrimination. Within limits, we may analogize from the *Hawkins*[81] case to the problem of moving away reasonably from the exclusionary rule; the Court should declare that the states are and shall be saddled with the unpopular exclusionary rule unless and until the states find a *bona fide* substitute for it which is acceptable to the Court. The standards for judging state substitutes for the rule would be the promise they offer (by the time any state plan reaches the Court it will have had at least a short period of operation and can thus be judged partially on previous performance) of accomplishing the twin objectives of punishing law officers who behave improperly and compensating innocent victims.

Of course, it is not only state legislatures but also the United States Congress which should be encouraged to enact alternatives to the exclusionary rule along the lines of the proposal made here.

Substituting alternatives to suppression of evidence makes the future uncertain, but such an uncertainty seems the only way to move us away from our addiction to suppression of illegally obtained evidence; like most addictions, this one has worked out badly.

Notes

1. *Student Comments: The Tort Alternative to the Exclusionary Rule in Search and Seizure*, 63 J. of Crim. L., C. & P.S. 256, 258 (1972).

2. *Grievance Response Mechanisms for Police Misconduct*, 55 Va. L. Rev. 909, 928 (1969). This Note considers "whether existing institutions are capable of affording an effective remedy against police misconduct and whether additional mechanisms should be established." 914. It discusses both existing and potential judicial and administrative machinery for dealing with physical abuse, harassment, and discourtesy by the police. The Note concludes that an effective system for dealing with police misconduct "might emerge from a hybrid of the ombudsman and the civilian review board." 947.

3. For discussions of external review mechanisms overseeing the work of the police, see: *Reviewing Civilian Complaints of Police Misconduct— Some Answers and More Questions*, 48 Temp. L. Q. 89, esp. 116-18 (1974); Hudson, *Police Review Boards and Police Accountability*, 36 Law & Contemp. Prob. 515 (1971); Schwartz, *Complaints Against the Police: Experience of the Community Rights Division of the Philadelphia District Attorney's Office*, 118 U. Pa. L. Rev. 1023 (1970); *Police Disciplinary Procedures: A Denial of Dur Process*, 7 John Marshall J. 111 (1973).

4. *Grievance Response Mechanisms*, footnote 2, *supra*, 939.

5. *Ibid.*, 938.

6. *Ibid.*, 938, note 159.

7. *Ibid.*

8. *Ibid.*, 911.

9. *Ibid.*, 939.

10. *Ibid.*, 940.

11. *Ibid.*, 941-42.

12. *Ibid.*, 942.

13. *Ibid.*

14. *Ibid.*

15. *Ibid.*, 942-43.

16. *Ibid.*, 943.

17. *Ibid.*, 943-44.

18. On the subject of civil actions, see *Student Comments, The Tort Alternative to the Exclusionary Rule in Search and Seizure*, 63 J. Crim. L., C. and P.S. 256 (1972); *The Federal Injunction as a Remedy for Unconstitutional Police Conduct*, 78 Yale L.J. 143 (1968); *Grievance*

Response Mechanisms for Police Misconduct, 55 Va. L. Rev. 909
(1969); *Note: Lawless Law Enforcement,* 4 Loyola U.L. Rev. (LA)
161 (1971); Ginger and Bell, *Police Misconduct Litigation–Plaintiffs'
Remedies,* 15 Am. Jur. Trials 55 (1968); Levin, *An Alternative to the
Exclusionary Rule for Fourth Amendment Violations,* 58 Judicature
75 (1974); LaPrade, *An Alternative to the Exclusionary Rule Presently
Administered Under the Fourth Amendment,* 48 Conn. B. J. 100
(1974).

19. *Grievance Response Mechanisms,* footnote 2, *supra,* 916-20.
20. We have reference here to the Community Legal Services Office of the Office of Economic Opportunity.
21. On the advisability of government liability, see Levin, footnote 18, *supra,* esp. 77 (1974).
22. LaPrade, footnote 18, *supra,* 109.
23. *Ibid.*
24. See *Grievance Response Mechanisms,* footnote 2, *supra,* 915-16.
25. Davis, *An Approach to Legal Control of the Police,* 52 Tex. L. Rev. 703, 717-22 (1974).
26. *Grievance Response Mechanisms,* footnote 2, *supra,* 919.
27. Davis, footnote 25, *supra,* 718.
28. 403 U.S. 388 (1971).
29. Oaks, *Studying the Exclusionary Rule in Search and Seizure,* 37 U. Chi. L. Rev. 665, 673, note 37 (1970).
30. *Student Comments,* footnote 1, *supra,* 263-64.
31. *Ibid.,* 265.
32. *Grievance Response Mechanisms,* footnote 2, *supra,* 921-23. The Federal Courts are in some disagreement as to the standard of liability to be applied in police misconduct cases.
33. *Ibid.,* 917.
34. Smith, *The American Bar Association and Delivery of Legal Services: A General Overview,* 45 Penn. B.A. Q. 343 (1974); Halpern, *Public Interest Law–Its Past and Future,* 58 Judicature 118 (1974).
35. *Grievance Response Mechanisms,* footnote 2, *supra,* 916-20.
36. *Ibid.*
37. Footnote 34, *supra.*
38. *Grievance Response Mechanisms,* footnote 2, *supra,* 918.
39. *Ibid.,* 919.
40. Foote, *Tort Remedies for Police Violations of Individual Rights,* 39 Minn. L. Rev. 493, 500 (1955), in *Grievance Response Mechanisms,* footnote 2, *supra,* 919, note 49.

41. *Grievance Response Mechanisms*, footnote 2, *supra*, 919.

42. *Ibid.*, 921.

43. 42 U.S.C. 1983 (1964).

44. 365 U.S. 167 (1961).

45. *Ibid.*, 184.

46. *Grievance Response Mechanisms*, footnote 2, *supra*, 921.

47. *Ibid.*, 922.

48. Ginger and Bell, footnote 18, *supra*, 579.

49. 365 U.S. 167, 187 (1961).

50. *Ibid.*, at 183.

51. *Ibid.*, at 187-92.

52. Davis, footnote 25, *supra*, 721.

53. Ginger and Bell, footnote 18, *supra*, 579-90. Some of the reported cases are interim successes, subject to appellate reversal.

54. 253 F. Supp. 420 (1963).

55. 354 F. 2d 16 (1965), SD Cal #776-61-EC.

56. See also, *Caperci v. Huntoon*, 397 F. 2d 799 (1968).

57. Footnote 28, *supra*.

58. See, for example, *Lankford v. Gelston*, 364 F. 2d 197 (1966); *Wheeler v. Goodman*, 298 F. Supp. 935 (1969).

59. *Grievance Response Mechanisms*, footnote 2, *supra*, 929-35.

60. 367 U.S.643 (1961).

61. Oaks, footnote 29, *supra*, 753.

62. See for the argument concerning respect for the courts and law, Paulsen, *The Exclusionary Rule and Misconduct by the Police*, 52 J. Crim. L., C. and P.S. 255, 258-59 (1961); see also *Olmstead v. United States*, 277 U.S. 438, 485 (1928) (dissenting opinion); *Weeks v. United States*, 232 U.S. 388, 394 (1914); *Burdeau v. McDowell*, 256 U.S. 465, 477 (1921) (dissenting opinion). For the argument about government benefit from its wrongdoing, see *Silverthorne Lumber Co. v. United States*, 351 U.S. 385, 392 (1920). For a mention of both of these arguments, see *United States v. Calandra*, 414 U.S. 338, 357 (1974) (Brennan, J., dissenting).

63. *Bivens*, footnote 28, *supra*, 421.

64. *Ibid.*, 422-23.

65. *Boyd v. United States*, 116 U.S. 616 (1886).

66. *Weeks v. United States*, 232 U.S. 383 (1914).

67. S. 2657, introduced 10/6/71.

68. H.R. 13682.

69. Congressman McKay's bill was H.R. 17096, introduced 10/11/72; Senator Bentsen's was S. 881, introduced 2/15/73.

70. H.R. 10275, introduced 9/13/73 and H.R. 5628, introduced 3/26/75.

71. *Michigan v. Tucker,* 417 U.S. 433 (1974).

72. *Ibid.,* 446.

73. 43 L.W. 4918 (1975).

74. 413 U.S. 266 (1973).

75. Footnote 73, *supra,* 4922. See also *Stone v. Powell,* 44 L.W. 5313, 5334 (1976) (White, J., dissenting).

76. Footnote 60, *supra.*

77. *Ibid.*

78. See for example, *Brown v. Board of Education of Topeka,* 347 U.S. 483 (1954) and 349 U.S. 294 (1955); *Swann v. Charlotte-Mecklenburg Board of Education,* 402 U.S. 1 (1971).

79. 413 U.S. 15 (1973).

80. 437 F. 2d. 1286 (1971). I would like to thank W. David Curtiss, Professor of Law at Cornell University, for bringing this case to my attention.

81. *Ibid.*

Chief Justice Burger's Dissent in *Bivens*

Mr. Chief Justice Burger, dissenting.

I dissent from today's holding which judicially creates a damage remedy not provided for by the Constitution and not enacted by Congress. We would more surely preserve the important values of the doctrine of separation of powers—and perhaps get a better result—by recommending a solution to the Congress as the branch of government in which the Constitution has vested the legislative power. Legislation is the business of the Congress, and it has the facilities and competence for that task—as we do not. Professor Thayer, speaking of the limits on judicial power, albeit in another context, had this to say:

> And if it be true that the holders of legislative power are careless or evil, yet the constitutional duty of the court remains untouched; it cannot rightly attempt to protect the people, by undertaking a function not its own. On the other hand, by adhering rigidly to its own duty, the court will help, as nothing else can, to fix the spot where responsibility lies, and to bring down on that precise locality the thunderbolt of popular condemnation. . . . For that course—the true course of judicial duty always—will powerfully help to bring the people and their representatives to a sense of their own responsibility.[1]

This case has significance far beyond its facts and its holding. For more than 55 years this Court has enforced a rule under which evidence of undoubted reliability and probative value has been suppressed and excluded from criminal cases whenever it was obtained in violation of the Fourth Amendment. *Weeks v. United States,* 232 U.S. 383, 58 L. Ed. 652, 34 S. Ct. 341 (1914); *Boyd v. United States,* 116 U.S. 616, 633, 29 L. Ed. 746,

752, 6 S. Ct. 524 (1886) (dictum). This rule was extended to the States in *Mapp v. Ohio*, 367 U.S. 643, 6 L. Ed. 2d 1081, 81 S. Ct. 1684, 84 A.L.R. 2d 933 (1961).[2] The rule has rested on a theory that suppression of evidence in these circumstances was imperative to deter law enforcement authorities from using improper methods to obtain evidence.

The deterrence theory underlying the suppression doctrine, or exclusionary rule, has a certain appeal in spite of the high price society pays for such a drastic remedy. Notwithstanding its plausibility, many judges and lawyers and some of our most distinguished legal scholars have never quite been able to escape the force of Cardozo's statement of the doctrine's anomalous result:

> The criminal is to go free because the constable has blundered. . . . A room is searched against the law, and the body of a murdered man is found. . . . The privacy of the home has been infringed, and the murderer goes free. *People v. Defore*, 242 N.Y. 13, 21, 23-4, 150 N.E. 585, 587, 588 (1926).[3]

The plurality opinion in *Irvine v. California*, 347 U.S. 128, 136, 98 L. Ed. 561, 571, 74 S. Ct. 381 (1954), catalogued the doctrine's defects:

> Rejection of the evidence does nothing to punish the wrong-doing official, while it may, and likely will, release the wrong-doing defendant. It deprives society of its remedy against one lawbreaker because he has been pursued by another. It protects one against whom incriminating evidence is discovered, but does nothing to protect innocent persons who are the victims of illegal but fruitless searches.

From time to time members of the Court, recognizing the validity of these protests, have articulated varying alternative justifications for the suppression of important evidence in a criminal trial. Under one of these alternative theories the rule's foundation is shifted to the "sporting contest" thesis that the government must "play the game fairly" and cannot be allowed to profit from its own illegal acts. *Olmstead v. United States*, 277 U.S. 438, 469, 471, 72 L. Ed. 944, 952, 953, 48 S. Ct. 564, 66 A.L.R. 376 (1928) (dissenting opinions); see *Terry v. Ohio*, 392 U.S. 1, 13, 20 L. Ed. 2d 889, 901, 88 S. Ct. 1868 (1968). But the exclusionary rule does not ineluctably flow from a desire to ensure that government plays the "game" according to the rules. If an effective alternative remedy is available, concern for official observance of the law does not require adherence to the exclusionary rule. Nor is it easy to understand how a court can be thought to endorse a violation of the Fourth Amendment by allowing illegally seized evidence to be introduced against a defendant if an effective remedy is provided against the government.

The exclusionary rule has also been justified on the theory that the relationship between the Self-Incrimination Clause of the Fifth Amendment and the Fourth Amendment requires the suppression of evidence seized in violation of the latter. *Boyd v. United States, supra,* at 633, 29 L. Ed. at 752 (dictum); *Wolf v. Colorado,* 338 U.S. 25, 47, 48, 93 L. Ed. 1782, 1795, 1796, 69 S. Ct. 1359 (1949) (Rutledge, J., dissenting); *Mapp v. Ohio, supra,* at 661-66, 6 L. Ed. 2d at 1093-96, 84 A.L.R. 2d 933 (Black, J., concurring).

Even ignoring, however, the decisions of this Court that have held that the Fifth Amendment applies only to "testimonial" disclosures, *United States v. Wade,* 388 U.S. 218, 221-23, 18 L. Ed. 2d 1149, 1153-55, 87 S. Ct. 1926 (1967); *Schmerber v. California,* 384 U.S. 757, 764 and n 8, 16 L. Ed. 2d 908, 916, 86 S. Ct. 1826 (1966), it seems clear that the Self-Incrimination Clause does not protect a person from the seizure of evidence that is incriminating. It protects a person only from being the conduit by which the police acquire evidence. Mr. Justice Holmes once put it succinctly, "A party is privileged from producing the evidence but not from its production." *Johnson v. United States,* 288 U.S. 457, 458, 57 L. Ed. 919, 920, 33 S. Ct. 572 (1913).

It is clear, however, that neither of these theories undergirds the decided cases in this Court. Rather the exclusionary rule has rested on the deterrent rationale—the hope that law enforcement officials would be deterred from unlawful searches and seizures if the illegally seized, albeit trustworthy, evidence was suppressed often enough and the courts persistently enough deprived them of any benefits they might have gained from their illegal conduct.

This evidentiary rule is unique to American jurisprudence. Although the English and Canadian legal systems are highly regarded, neither has adopted our rule. See Martin, *The Exclusionary Rule Under Foreign Law— Canada,* 52 J. Crim. L. C. & P. S. 271, 272 (1961); Williams, *The Exclusionary Rule Under Foreign Law—England,* 52 J. Crim. L. C. & P. S. 272 (1961).

I do not question the need for some remedy to give meaning and teeth to the constitutional guarantees against unlawful conduct by government officials. Without some effective sanction, these protections would constitute little more than rhetoric. Beyond doubt the conduct of some officials requires sanctions as cases like Irvine indicate. But the hope that this objective could be accomplished by the exclusion of reliable evidence from criminal trials was hardly more than a wistful dream. Although I would hesitate to abandon it until some meaningful substitute is developed, the history of the suppression doctrine demonstrates that it is both conceptually sterile and practically ineffective in accomplishing its stated objective. This is illustrated by the paradox that an unlawful act against a totally innocent person—such as petitioner claims to be—has been left without an effective remedy, and hence the Court finds it necessary now—55 years later—to construct a remedy of its own.

Some clear demonstration of the benefits and effectiveness of the exclusionary rule is required to justify it in view of the high price it extracts from society—the release of countless guilty criminals. See Allen, *Federalism and the Fourth Amendment: A Requiem for Wolf*, 1961 Sup. Ct. Rev. 1, 33 n 172. But there is no empirical evidence to support the claim that the rule actually deters illegal conduct of law enforcement officials. Oaks, *Studying the Exclusionary Rule in Search and Seizure*, 37 U. Chi. L. Rev. 665, 667 (1970).

There are several reasons for this failure. The rule does not apply any direct sanction to the individual official whose illegal conduct results in the exclusion of evidence in a criminal trial. With rare exceptions law enforcement agencies do not impose direct sanctions on the individual officer responsible for a particular judicial application of the suppression doctrine. *Id.*, at 710. Thus there is virtually nothing done to bring about a change in his practices. The immediate sanction triggered by the application of the rule is visited upon the prosecutor whose case against a criminal is either weakened or destroyed. The doctrine deprives the police in no real sense; except that apprehending wrongdoers is their business, police have no more stake in successful prosecutions than prosecutors or the public.

The suppression doctrine vaguely assumes that law enforcement is a monolithic governmental enterprise. For example, the dissenters in *Wolf v. Colorado, supra*, at 44, 93 L. Ed. at 1794, argued that:

> Only by exclusion can we impress upon the zealous *prosecutor* that violation of the Constitution will do him no good. And only when that point is driven home can the *prosecutor* be expected to emphasize the importance of observing the constitutional demands in *his instructions to the police.*

But the prosecutor who loses his case because of police misconduct is not an official in the police department; he can rarely set in motion any corrective action or administrative penalties. Moreover, he does not have control or direction over police procedures or police actions that lead to the exclusion of evidence. It is the rare exception when a prosecutor takes part in arrests, searches, or seizures so that he can guide police action.

Whatever educational effect the rule conceivably might have in theory is greatly diminished in fact by the realities of law enforcement work. Policemen do not have the time, inclination, or training to read and grasp the nuances of the appellate opinions that ultimately define the standards of conduct they are to follow. The issues that these decisions resolve often admit of neither easy nor obvious answers, as sharply divided courts on what is or is not "reasonable" amply demonstrate.[4] Nor can judges, in all candor, forget that opinions sometimes lack helpful clarity.

The presumed educational effect of judicial opinions is also reduced by the long time lapse—often several years—between the original police action and its final judicial evaluation. Given a policeman's pressing responsibilities, it would be surprising if he ever becomes aware of the final result after such a delay. Finally, the exclusionary rule's deterrent impact is diluted by the fact that there are large areas of police activity that do not result in criminal prosecutions—hence the rule has virtually no applicability and no effect in such situations. Oaks, *supra,* at 720-24.

Today's holding seeks to fill one of the gaps of the suppression doctrine— at the price of impinging on the legislative and policy functions that the Constitution vests in Congress. Nevertheless, the holding serves the useful purpose of exposing the fundamental weaknesses of the suppression doctrine. Suppressing unchallenged truth has set guilty criminals free but demonstrably has neither deterred deliberate violations of the Fourth Amendment nor decreased those errors in judgment that will inevitably occur given the pressures inherent in police work having to do with serious crimes.

Although unfortunately ineffective, the exclusionary rule has increasingly been characterized by a single, monolithic, and drastic judicial response to all official violations of legal norms. Inadvertent errors of judgment that do not work any grave injustice will inevitably occur under the pressure of police work. These honest mistakes have been treated in the same way as deliberate and flagrant Irvine-type violations of the Fourth Amendment. For example, in *Miller v. United States,* 357 U.S. 301, 309-10, 2 L. Ed. 2d 1332, 1338, 78 S. Ct. 1190 (1958), reliable evidence was suppressed because of a police officer's failure to say a "few more words" during the arrest and search of a known narcotics peddler.

This Court's decision announced today in *Coolidge v. New Hampshire,* 403 U.S. 443, 29 L. Ed. 2d 564, 91 S. Ct. 2022, dramatically illustrates the extent to which the doctrine represents a mechanically inflexible response to widely varying degrees of police error and the resulting high price that society pays. I dissented in Coolidge primarily because I do not believe the Fourth Amendment had been violated. Even on the Court's contrary premise, however, whatever violation occurred was surely insufficient in nature and extent to justify the drastic result dictated by the suppression doctrine. A fair trial by jury has resolved doubts as to Coolidge's guilt. But now his conviction on retrial is placed in serious question by the remand for a new trial—years after the crime—in which evidence that the New Hampshire courts found relevant and reliable will be withheld from the jury's consideration. It is hardly surprising that such results are viewed with incomprehension by nonlawyers in this country and lawyers, judges, and legal scholars the world over.

Freeing either a tiger or a mouse in a schoolroom is an illegal act, but no rational person would suggest that these two acts should be punished in the same way. From time to time judges have occasion to pass on regulations governing police procedures. I wonder what would be the judicial response to a police order authorizing "shoot to kill" with respect to every fugitive. It is easy to predict our collective wrath and outrage. We, in common with all rational minds, would say that the police response must relate to the gravity and need; that a "shoot" order might conceivably be tolerable to prevent the escape of a convicted killer but surely not for a car thief, a pickpocket or a shoplifter.

I submit that society has at least as much right to expect rationally graded responses from judges in place of the universal "capital punishment" we inflict on all evidence when police error is shown in its acquisition. See A.L.I., *Model Code of Pre-Arraignment Procedure* § SS 8.02(2), p. 23 (Tent. Draft No. 4, 1971), reprinted in the Appendix to this opinion. Yet for over 55 years, and with increasing scope and intensity as today's Coolidge holding shows, our legal system has treated vastly dissimilar cases as if they were the same. Our adherence to the exclusionary rule, our resistance to change, and our refusal even to acknowledge the need for effective enforcement mechanisms bring to mind Holmes' well-known statement:

> It is revolting to have no better reason for a rule of law than that so it was laid down in the time of Henry IV. It is still more revolting if the grounds upon which it was laid down have vanished long since, and the rule simply persists from blind imitation of the past. Holmes, *The Path of the Law,* 10 Harv. L. Rev. 457, 469 (1897).

In characterizing the suppression doctrine as an anomalous and ineffective mechanism with which to regulate law enforcement, I intend no reflection on the motivation of those members of this Court who hoped it would be a means of enforcing the Fourth Amendment. Judges cannot be faulted for being offended by arrests, searches, and seizures that violate the Bill of Rights or statutes intended to regulate public officials. But we can and should be faulted for clinging to an unworkable and irrational concept of law. My criticism is that we have taken so long to find better ways to accomplish these desired objectives. And there are better ways.

Instead of continuing to enforce the suppression doctrine inflexibly, rigidly, and mechanically, we should view it as one of the experimental steps in the great tradition of the common law and acknowledge its shortcomings. But in the same spirit we should be prepared to discontinue what the experience of over half a century has shown neither deters errant officers nor affords a remedy to the totally innocent victims of official misconduct.

I do not propose, however, that we abandon the suppression doctrine until some meaningful alternative can be developed. In a sense our legal system has become the captive of its own creation. To overrule Weeks and Mapp, even assuming the Court was now prepared to take that step, could raise yet new problems. Obviously the public interest would be poorly served if law enforcement officials were suddenly to gain the impression, however erroneous, that all constitutional restraints on police had somehow been removed—that an open season on "criminals" had been declared. I am concerned lest some such mistaken impression might be fostered by a flat overruling of the suppression doctrine cases. For years we have relied upon it as the exclusive remedy for unlawful official conduct; in a sense we are in a situation akin to the narcotics addict whose dependence on drugs precludes any drastic or immediate withdrawal of the supposed prop, regardless of how futile its continued use may be.

Reasonable and effective substitutes can be formulated if Congress would take the lead, as it did for example in 1946 in the Federal Tort Claims Act. I see no insuperable obstacle to the elimination of the suppression doctrine if Congress would provide some meaningful and effective remedy against unlawful conduct by government officials.

The problems of both error and deliberate misconduct by law enforcement officials call for a workable remedy. Private damage actions against individual police officers concededly have not adequately met this requirement, and it would be fallacious to assume today's work of the Court in creating a remedy will really accomplish its stated objective. There is some validity to the claims that juries will not return verdicts against individual officers except in those unusual cases where the violation has been flagrant or where the error has been complete, as in the arrest of the wrong person or the search of the wrong house. There is surely serious doubt, for example, that a drug peddler caught packaging his wares will be able to arouse much sympathy in a jury on the ground that the police officer did not announce his identity and purpose fully or because he failed to utter a "few more words." See *Miller v. United States, supra.* Jurors may well refuse to penalize a police officer at the behest of a person they believe to be a "criminal" and probably will not punish an officer for honest errors of judgment. In any event an actual recovery depends on finding nonexempt assets of the police officer from which a judgment can be satisfied.

I conclude, therefore, that an entirely different remedy is necessary but it is one that in my view is as much beyond judicial power as the step the Court takes today. Congress should develop an administrative or quasi-judicial remedy against the government itself to afford compensation and restitution for persons whose Fourth Amendment rights have been violated. The venerable doctrine of respondeat superior in our tort law provides an entirely appropriate conceptual basis for this remedy. If, for example, a security guard privately employed by a department store commits an assault or other tort on a customer such as an improper search, the victim has a simple and obvious remedy—an action for money damages against the guard's employer, the department store. W. Prosser, *The Law of Torts* § 68, pp. 470-80 (3d ed., 1964).[5] Such a statutory scheme would have the added advantage of providing some remedy to the completely innocent persons who are sometimes the victims of illegal police conduct—something that the suppression doctrine, of course, can never accomplish.

A simple structure would suffice.[6] For example, Congress could enact a statute along the following lines:

1. A waiver of sovereign immunity as to the illegal acts of law enforcement officials committed in the performance of assigned duties

2. The creation of a cause of action for damages sustained by any person aggrieved by conduct of governmental agents in violation of the Fourth Amendment or statutes regulating official conduct

3. The creation of a tribunal, quasi-judicial in nature or perhaps patterned after the United States Court of Claims, to adjudicate all claims under the statute

4. A provision that this statutory remedy is in lieu of the exclusion of evidence secured for use in criminal cases in violation of the Fourth Amendment

5. A provision directing that no evidence, otherwise admissible, shall be excluded from any criminal proceeding because of violation of the Fourth Amendment

I doubt that lawyers serving on such a tribunal would be swayed either by undue sympathy for officers or by the prejudice against "criminals" that has sometimes moved lay jurors to deny claims. In addition to awarding damages, the record of the police conduct that is condemned would undoubtedly become a relevant part of an officer's personnel file so that the need for additional training or disciplinary action could be identified or his future usefulness as a public official evaluated. Finally, appellate judicial review could be made available on much the same basis that it is now provided as to district courts and regulatory agencies. This would leave to the courts the ultimate responsibility for determining and articulating standards.

Once the constitutional validity of such a statute is established,[7] it can reasonably be assumed that the States would develop their own remedial systems on the federal model. Indeed there is nothing to prevent a State from enacting a comparable statutory scheme without waiting for the Congress. Steps along these lines would move our system toward more responsible law enforcement on the one hand and away from the irrational and drastic results of the suppression doctrine on the other. Independent of the alternative embraced in this dissenting opinion, I believe the time has come to reexamine the scope of the exclusionary rule and consider at least some narrowing of its thrust so as to eliminate the anomalies it has produced.

In a country that prides itself on innovation, inventive genius, and willingness to experiment, it is a paradox that we should cling for more than a half century to a legal mechanism that was poorly designed and never really worked. I can only hope that the Congress will manifest a willingness to view realistically the hard evidence of the half-century history of the suppression doctrine revealing thousands of cases in which the criminal was set free because the constable blundered and virtually no evidence that innocent victims of police error—such as petitioner claims to be—have been afforded meaningful redress.

Notes

1. J. Thayer, O. Holmes, & F. Frankfurter, John Marshall 88 (Phoenix ed., 1967).
2. The Court reached the issue of applying the Weeks doctrine to the States *sua sponte*.
3. What Cardozo suggested as an example of the potentially far-reaching consequences of the suppression doctrine was almost realized in *Killough v. United States,* 114 U.S. App. D.C. 305, 315 F2d 241 (1962).

4. For example, in a case arising under *Mapp, supra,* state judges at every
    level of the state judiciary may find the police conduct proper. On
    federal habeas corpus a district judge and a court of appeals might
    agree. Yet, in these circumstances, this Court, reviewing the case as
    much as 10 years later, might reverse by a narrow margin. In these
    circumstances it is difficult to conclude that the policeman has
    violated some rule that he should have known was a restriction on
    his authority.

5. Damage verdicts for such acts are often sufficient in size to provide an
    effective deterrent and stimulate employers to corrective action.

6. Electronic eavesdropping presents special problems. See 18 U.S.C. §§
    2510-20 (1964 ed., Supp. V).

7. Any such legislation should emphasize the interdependence between
    the waiver of sovereign immunity and the elimination of the judicially
    created exclusionary rule so that if the legislative determination to
    repudiate the exclusionary rule falls, the entire statutory scheme would
    fall.

The Comparative Question

The interested reader may well ask why more has not been said in a comparative context as to how other countries deal with the problem of police misbehavior. In fact, none of the Western European nations or Canada use police misconduct as the rationale for excluding otherwise probative evidence to the extent that this is done in the United States.[1] One of the most valuable recent comparative studies is that of James Spiotto,[2] who reports that Canadian law renders all probative evidence admissible and provides that citizens may bring a civil tort action against police officers alleged to have engaged in illegal conduct. Spiotto provides the reader with a good deal of helpful background by discussing the organization of police in Ontario Province and police-community relations in that province, and by reviewing the Canadian laws concerning search and seizure.

And yet the value of comparisons between Canada and the United States is limited; what is effective in Canada may not be in the United States. As Spiotto points out:

> Canadian officials do not think that Canada has a problem with illegal search and seizure . . . in Toronto, tort suits against the police for illegal search and seizure are less frequent than in Chicago. Police disciplinary actions against police for illegal search and seizure are virtually nonexistent in Toronto as compared to Chicago. The explanation for non-concern over the problem of illegal search and seizure might simply be that few illegal searches are made by Canadian police.[3]

Thus, it may be that Canadian police are simply better disciplined than their American counterparts. Spiotto notes that the crime rate in Toronto, especially that of violent crime, is substantially less than that in the United States, thus putting less pressure on the police to deal with crimes by illegal methods. In addition, Canada's problem with crime is not exacerbated by the level of racial tension experienced in the United States. Finally, it would seem that these factors which differentiate the Canadian law enforcement situation from the American are likewise present in the nations of Western Europe.

These differences render comparison of the American use of the exclusionary rule with Canadian and Western European reluctance to use it of limited value. If one were to hold up Canada or the Western European nations as examples of how some nations get along very well without the rule, the reply would be that, because the police are better disciplined in these nations and the crime rate lower, these countries have less need for an exclusionary rule than does the United States. These kinds of arguments render it difficult to make meaningful comparisons between our exclusionary rule and the methods of dealing with police misbehavior used in Canada and the Western European nations.

Notes

1. See Damaska, *Interrogation of Defendants in Yugoslavia,* 61 J. Crim. L., C. and P.S. 179-80, n. 68 (1970), for an annotated bibliography of the European literature showing that "the tenor of the Continental tradition is, of course, in favor of admissibility . . . ." *Ibid.*; *The Exclusionary Rule Regarding Illegally Seized Evidence: An International Symposium,* 52 J. Crim. L., C. and P.S. 245-92 (1961); and Spiotto, *The Search and Seizure Problem—Two Approaches: The Canadian Tort Remedy and the American Exclusionary Rule,* 1 J. Police Sci. and Ad. 36 (1973).
2. Footnote 1, *supra.*
3. *Ibid.,* at 48.

Bibliography

Books

Canadian Committee on Correction, *Toward Unity: Criminal Justice and Corrections* (Ottawa: Queens Printer, 1969).

Crime in the Nation's Five Largest Cities, Law Enforcement Assistance Administration, U. S. Dept. of Justice (Washington, D.C.: U.S. Government Printing Office, 1974).

Hindelang, *et al., Sourcebook on Criminal Justice Statistics, 1973,* Law Enforcement Assistance Administration, U.S. Dept. of Justice (Washington, D.C.: U.S. Government Printing Office, 1973).

Fred Inbau, James Thompson, and Claude Sowle, *Cases and Comments on Criminal Justice* (Mineola, N.Y.: Foundation Press, 1968).

Wayne Lafave, *Arrest: The Decision to Take a Suspect Into Custody* (Boston: Little Brown, 1965).

William Lockhart, Yale Kamisar, and Jesse Choper, *The American Constitution: Cases and Materials* (St. Paul, Minn.: West Publishing Co., 1970).

Frank Miller, *Prosecution: The Decision to Charge a Suspect With a Crime* (Boston: Little Brown, 1969).

Norval Morris and Gordon Hawkins, *The Honest Politician's Guide to Crime Control* (Chicago: University of Chicago Press, 1970).

Jerome Skolnik, *Justice Without Trial* (New York: Wiley, 1966).

John Wigmore, *A Treatise on the Anglo-American System of Evidence in Trials at Common Law* (Boston: Little Brown, 1940).

James Wilson, *Varieties of Police Behavior* (Cambridge, Mass.: Harvard University Press, 1968).

Articles

Albert W. Alschuler, *The Prosecutor's Role in Plea Bargaining,* 36 U. Chi. L. Rev. 50 (1968).

Edward Barrett, *Exclusion of Evidence Obtained by Illegal Searches, A Comment on People vs. Cahan,* 43 Calif. L. Rev. 565 (1965).

109

Edward Barrett, *Personal Rights, Property Rights and the Fourth Amendment*, 1960 Sup. Ct. Rev. 46.

Dale W. Broedes, *Wong Sun v. United States: A Study in Faith and Hope*, 42 Neb. L. Rev. 483 (1963).

Robert E. Burns, *Mapp v. Ohio: An All-American Mistake*, 19 DePaul L. Rev. 80 (1969).

Bradley C. Canon, *Is the Exclusionary Rule in Failing Health? Some New Data and a Plea Against A Precipitous Conclusion*, 62 Ky. L. J. 681 (1973-74).

J. L. Clendenning, *Police Power and Civil Liberties*, 40 Osgood Hall L. J. 174 (1974).

Comment, Search & Seizure in Illinois: Enforcement of the Constitutional Right of Privacy, 47 Nw. U. L. Rev. 493 (1952).

William J. Cox, *The Decline of the Exclusionary Rule: An Alternative to Injustice*, 4 Sw. U. L. Rev. 68 (1972).

Critique: On the Limitations of Empirical Evaluations of the Exclusionary Rule: A Critique of the Spiotto Research and United States v. Calandra, 69 Nw. U. L. Rev. 740 (1974).

Samuel Dash, *Cracks in the Foundation of Criminal Justice*, 41 Ill. L. Rev. 385 (1951).

Kenneth C. Davis, *An Approach to Legal Control of the Police*, 52 Tex. L. Rev. 703 (1974).

The Exclusionary Rule Regarding Illegally Seized Evidence: An International Symposium, 52 J. Crim. L., C. and P. S. 245-92 (1961).

The Federal Injunction as a Remedy for Unconstitutional Police Actions, 78 Yale L. J. 143 (1968).

Caleb Foote, *Tort Remedies for Police Violations of Individual Rights*, 39 Minn. L. Rev. 493 (1955).

Henry Friendly, *The Bill of Rights as a Code of Criminal Procedure*, 53 Calif. L. Rev. 929 (1965).

Ann Fagan Ginger and Louis Bell, *Police Misconduct Litigation—Plaintiffs' Remedies*, 15 Am. Jur. Trials 555 (1968).

Grievance Response Mechanisms for Police Misconduct, 55 Va. L. Rev. 909 (1969).

Charles R. Halpern, *Public Interest Law—Its Past and Future*, 58 Judicature 118 (1974).

James R. Hudson, *Police Review Boards and Police Accountability*, 36 L. and Contemp. Prob. 515 (1971).

Fred E. Inbau, *Restrictions in the Law of Interrogations and Confessions*, Nw. U. L. Rev. 77 (1958).

Yale Kamisar, *Wolf and Lustig, Ten Years Later: Illegal State Evidence in State and Federal Courts*, 43 Minn. L. Rev. 1083 (1959).

John Kaplan, *The Limits of the Exclusionary Rule,* 26 Stan. L. Rev. 1027 (1974).

Michael P. Katz, *The Supreme Court and the State: An Inquiry into Mapp v. Ohio in North Carolina,* 45 N.C.L. Rev. (1966).

Edmund W. Kitch, *The Supreme Court's Possessive Code of Criminal Procedure,* 1969 Sup. Ct. Rev. 157.

Wayne R. Lafave, *Improving Police Performance Through the Exclusionary Rule* (pts 1 and 2), 30 Mo. L. Rev. 391 (1965).

Wayne R. Lafave and Frank Remington, *Controlling the Police: The Judge's Role in Making and Reviewing Law Enforcement Decisions,* 63 Mich. L. Rev. 987 (1965).

Carter LaPrade, *An Alternative to the Exclusionary Rule Presently Administered under the Fourth Amendment,* 48 Conn. B. J. 100 (1974).

Lawless Law Enforcement, 4 Loyola U. L. Rev. (LA) 161 (1971).

Harvey Robert Levin, *An Alternative to the Exclusionary Rule for Fourth Amendment Violations,* 58 Judicature 75 (1974).

J. Arthur Martin, *The Exclusionary Rule Under Foreign Law: Canada,* in Claude Sowle (ed.), *Police Power and Individual Freedom* (Chicago: Aldine Pub. Co., 1962).

Stuart Nagel, *Testing the Effects of Excluding Illegally Obtained Evidence,* 1965 Wisc. L. Rev. 283.

Note: *Effect of Mapp v. Ohio on Police Search and Seizure Practice in Narcotics Cases,* 4 Colum. J. L. Soc. Prob. 87 (1968).

Dallin Oaks, *Studying the Exclusionary Rule in Search and Seizure,* 37 U. Chi. L. Rev. 665 (1970).

G. E. Parker, *The Extraordinary Power to Search & Seize and the Writ of Assistance,* 1 U.B.O.L. Rev. 688 (1963).

Monrad Paulsen, *The Exclusionary Rule and Misconduct by the Police,* 52 J. Crim. L., C. and P.S. 255 (1961).

William T. Plumb, Jr., *Illegal Enforcement of the Law,* 24 Cornell L.Q. 337 (1939).

Police Disciplinary Procedures: A Denial of Due Process, 7 John Marshall J. 111 (1973).

Reviewing Civilian Complaints of Police Misconduct—Some Answers and More Questions, 48 Temp. L. Q. 89 (1974).

Kenneth B. Satlin, *An Alternative to the Exclusionary Rule,* 26 JAG J. 255 (1972).

Walter Schaefer, *The Fourteenth Amendment and the Sanctity of the Person,* 64 Nw. U. L. Rev. 1 (1969).

Steven Schlesinger, *Witness Against Himself: The Fifth Amendment Self-Incrimination Clause As Public Policy,* 3 Claremont J. 55 (1975).

Thomas S. Schrock and Robert C. Welsh, *The Exclusionary Rule as a Constitutional Requirement,* 59 Minn. L. Rev. 251 (1974).

Louis B. Schwartz, *Complaints Against the Police: Experience of the Community Rights Division of the Philadelphia District Attorney's Office,* 118 U.Pa. L. Rev. 1023 (1970).

Chesterfield Smith, *The American Bar Association and Delivery of Legal Services: A General Overview,* 45 Penn. B. A. Q. 343 (1974).

James Spiotto, *Search and Seizure, An Empirical Study of the Exclusionary Rule and Its Alternatives,* 2 J. Legal Studies 243 (1973).

James Spiotto, *The Search and Seizure Problem: The Canadian Tort Remedy and the American Exclusionary Rule,* 1 J. Pol. Science and Ad. 36 (1973).

Student Comments, The Tort Alternative to the Exclusionary Rule in Search and Seizure, 63 J. Crim. L., C. and P.S. (1972).

John Barker Waite, *Judges and the Crime Burden,* 54 Mich. L. Rev. 168 (1955).

Paul C. Weiler, *The Control of Police Arrest Practices: Reflections of a Tort Lawyer,* in Allen M. Linden, *Studies in Canadian Tort Law* (Toronto: Butterworths, 1968).

Jack B. Weinstein, *Local Responsibility for Improvement of Search and Seizure Practices,* 34 Rocky Mt. L. Rev. 150 (1962).

John H. Wigmore, *Using Evidence Obtained by Illegal Search and Seizure,* 8 ABA J. 479 (1922).

Harvey Wingo, *Growing Disillusionment with the Exclusionary Rule,* 25 Sw. L. J. 573 (1971).

Case Index

Mapp v. Ohio, 367 U.S. 643 (1961), 1, 4, 7, 9, 12, 24, 26-31, 32-35, 39, 41, 44, 47, 50, 54-55, 57, 60-62, 66-67, 85, 91

McArthur v. Pennington, 253 F. Supp. 420 (1963), 83

Michigan v. Tucker, 417 U.S. 433 (1974), 8, 96

Miranda v. Arizona, 384 U.S. 436 (1966), 1

Monroe v. Pape, 365 U.S. 167 (1961), 82

Oregon v. Hass, 420 U.S. 714 (1975), 8

Olmstead v. United States, 277 U.S. 438 (1928), 95

Peters v. New York, 392 U.S. 40 (1968), 41

Rea v. United States, 350 U.S. 214 (1956), 24

Rochin v. California, 342 U.S. 165 (1952), 1, 7, 22-23, 43, 62

Sibron v. New York, 392 U.S. 40 (1968), 41

Silverthorne Lumber Co. v. United States, 251 U.S. 385 (1920), 31-32, 95

South Dakota v. Opperman, 44 L.W. 5294 (1976), 41, 69

Stanford v. Texas, 379 U.S. 476 (1965), 41

Stefanelli v. Minard, 342 U.S. 117 (1951), 21-22

Stone v. Powell, 44 L.W. 5313 (1976), 7-8, 12, 38-40, 67, 96

Swann v. Charlotte-Mecklenburg Board of Education, 402 U.S. 1 (1971), 96

Terry v. Ohio, 392 U.S. 1 (1968), 41

Trupiano v. United States, 334 U.S. 699 (1948), 41

United States v. Calandra, 414 U.S. 338 (1974), 4, 7, 12, 37-38, 46-47, 67, 84, 95

United States v. Janis, 44 L.W. 5303 (1976), 44

United States v. Peltier, 43 L.W. 4918 (1975), 90

United States v. Rabinowitz, 339 U.S. 56 (1950), 41

United States v. Santana, 44 L.W. 4970 (1976), 41, 68

United States v. Watson, 44 L.W. 4112 (1976), 41, 68

Warden v. Hayden, 387 U.S. 294 (1967), 41

Weeks v. United States, 232 U.S. 383 (1914), 7, 12, 17-21, 27-28, 30-31, 88, 95

Wheeler v. Goodman, 298 F. Supp. 935 (1969), 95

Wolf v. Colorado, 388 U.S. 25 (1949), 7, 9, 12, 19-23, 25-30, 35, 42, 60

Wolff v. Rice, 44 L.W. 5313 (1976), 8, 12, 38-40

Wong Sun v. United States, 371 U.S. 471 (1963), 12, 31-32, 41, 45

Name Index

Alschuler, Albert W., 68
Ban, Michael, 54-55
Barrett, Edward, 8, 64, 68
Bell, Louis, 83, 94-95
Bentsen, Lloyd, 88-89, 96
Berman, Julius, 44
Black, Hugo L., 41
Bradley, Joseph P., 14-17, 49, 68
Brandeis, Louis D., 19, 32, 42,
  60, 67
Brennan, William J., 32, 36, 38,
  40, 46, 67, 95
Broedes, Dale W., 45
Burger, Warren E., 5, 36, 58, 62,
  66, 87-88
Burns, Robert E., 8, 67
Camden, Lord, 15
Canon, Bradley C., 9, 54-55, 65
Choper, Jesse, 42
Clark, Tom C., 27-30, 33-35, 50,
  60
Cox, William J., 8
Curtiss, W. David, 96
Dash, Samuel, 66
Davis, Kenneth C., 79, 94-95
Day, William R., 18
Douglas, William O., 24, 38
Elliot, Ward, 8
Foote, Caleb, 81, 94
Frankfurter, Felix, 19-20, 22-23, 26,
  28-29, 44
Friendly, Henry, 8
Ginger, Ann Fagan, 83, 94-95
Halpern, Charles R., 94

Harlan, John M., 29-31, 44
Hawkins, Gordon, 8
Hindelang, Michael J., 8
Hogan, Lawrence, 88-89
Holmes, Oliver W., 19, 31-32, 60
Hudson, James R., 93
Inbau, Fred E., 8, 58, 67
Jackson, Robert H., 57
Kamisar, Yale, 42, 68
Kaplan, John, 67
Katz, Michael P., 65
Kitch, Edmund W., 68
Lafave, Wayne, 8, 56, 66-67
LaPrade, Carter, 94
Levin, Harvey Robert, 94
Lockhart, William, 42
McKay, Gunn, 88-89, 96
Marshall, John, 93
Marshall, Thurgood, 38, 40
Miller, Frank, 56
Miller, Samuel F., 16-17, 42
Morris, Norval, 8
Murphy, Frank, 9, 21, 43, 60, 67
Nagel, Stuart, 65
Oaks, Dallin H., 2, 7-8, 51-52, 55,
  58-59, 61, 63-68, 85, 94-95
Oberst, Paul, 44
Paulsen, Monrad, 95
Peterson, Virgil, 61
Plumb, William T., Jr., 8
Powell, Lewis F., 37, 39
Rehnquist, William H., 90
Remington, Frank, 8, 67
Rutledge, John, 9, 21

115